SO-AYC-023

New Poems
from the
Third Coast

Livonia Public Library
ALFRED NOBLE BRANCH
32901 PLYMOUTH ROAD
Livonia, Michigan 48150-1793
421-6600
LIVN #19

811.54
N

New Poems
from the
Third Coast

CONTEMPORARY MICHIGAN POETRY

Edited by
Michael Delp, Conrad Hilberry, and Josie Kearns

Foreword by Donald Hall

Livonia Public Library
ALFRED NOBLE BRANCH
32901 PLYMOUTH ROAD
Livonia, Michigan 48150-1793
421-6600
LIVN #19

Wayne State University Press   Detroit

3 9082 08594 5650

Great Lakes Books

A complete listing of the books in this series can be found at the back of this volume.

Philip P. Mason, Editor
Department of History, Wayne State University

Dr. Charles K. Hyde, Associate Editor
Department of History, Wayne State University

Copyright © 2000 by Wayne State University Press,
Detroit, Michigan 48201. All rights are reserved.
No part of this book may be reproduced without formal permission.
Manufactured in the United States of America.
04 03 02 01 00   5 4 3 2

Library of Congress Cataloging-in-Publication Data

New poems from the third coast : contemporary Michigan poetry / edited by Michael
Delp, Conrad Hilberry, and Josie Kearns.
    p. cm.
  ISBN 0-8143-2796-6 (alk. paper) -- ISBN 0-8143-2797-4 (pbk. : alk. paper)
    1. American poetry--Michigan. 2. American poetry--20th century. 3. Michigan--Poetry.
  I. Delp, Michael. II. Hilberry, Conrad. III. Kearns, Josie, 1954-

PS571.M5 N49 2000
811'.540809774--dc21
                                                                      00-025123

JAN 0 3 2002

See page 361 for acknowledgments of permission to reprint the poems in this volume.

Contents

Foreword

Donald Hall

Some poets here I have known for decades. Some I first read last week. Some are old students. Some have MacArthurs. It would be invidious to comment or list or quote, from a volume of such substance, unless one were asserting a Michigan style. Thank heaven there is no Michigan style. We find in this collection—as we would, I think, in a volume well-collected from Ohio or Illinois—confirmation of an astonishing reality: there has never been so much poetry happening in the United States, poems that range from expert competence to brilliance.

When I moved to Michigan in 1957, poetry was marginal in this state and in this country. Even at the millennium, its audience will not equal the NFL's, but in forty years poetry has become more prominent in Michigan and elsewhere. Late in the 1950s, the poetry reading was rare. Now, how many take place in Michigan alone, every week or every night? The poetry reading started things, and led the way to more magazines, more books, and more copies of books, MFA programs by the gross, and the widespread teaching of poetry writing in schools and colleges.

Of course, quantity says nothing about quality. At any time in history, doubtless the majority of poetry written and published is poor stuff, or will look like poor stuff forty years later. But, as this anthology shows, there are in Michigan many, many poets of distinct ability—who make original images, clean diction, rhythm and sound to connect with the body: who make poems that become complex engines of thought and feeling.

The growth of poetry is a counterforce—and a response—to our culture of numbers and information, of digits and commerce. We read and write poems so that our psyches can speak to each other with intelligence in the language of feeling, acknowledging the multiplicity and contradiction of each human life.

The quantity of our poetry, however, makes for difficulties in publication, and in judgment for judges. Recently I judged a contest to which poets submitted seventeen hundred poems. I had agreed to read thirty, not knowing that thirty poems would be such a tiny percentage of the whole. There were first readers I didn't know, who lived far away. It is perfectly possible, even probable, that if I had had the time, energy, and patience to read seventeen hundred poems, I would have given first prize to a poem not among my thirty.

Although there are more prizes than ever—book publication, cash, other forms of recognition—large numbers allow the Lottery Effect to take over. Years back, when forty people applied for a fellowship, the judge or judges could feel reasonably confident of judgment. When eight hundred poets apply for the same thing, judgment comes to resemble pulling names out of a hat. Nor do we have guidance from critics. As the quantity of poetry has increased, the quality and quantity of public discourse about poetry have dwindled. A few decades ago, a well-known poet might be published in an edition of seven hundred and fifty copies, and be reviewed by Louise Bogan in the *New Yorker*, Conrad Aiken in the *New Republic,* and Malcolm Cowley in the *Nation*. Now a poet of similar fame will be published in a first edition of seven thousand and go without a review in any national publication.

Because of their numbers, poets tend to gather themselves into groups, perhaps with geographical boundaries, to make a smaller pool in which good fish are more visible. We have the Los Angeles poets, poets of the Northwest, Minnesota poets . . . These assemblages are not regionalism; they are an effort toward community. Poets get to know each other. (It's little known outside the literary world that poets thrive by helping each other out. We all know some poets who would achieve eminence by murdering all others, but by and large poets are not opera singers.) Michigan is a large state, and the size of this book confirms the largeness of its poetic community. It also serves that community by the quality of the work chosen.

Wilmot, New Hampshire
23 July 1998

Preface

In 1976, Wayne State University Press published *The Third Coast: Contemporary Michigan Poetry,* an anthology that offered a sample of the best poetry being written at that moment in the state. The book was well received, widely read—and it became important over the years as a reminder of who the Michigan poets were in that decade and what sorts of images and ideas emerged in their work. A second *Third Coast* anthology appeared in 1988, with some of the same poets but with many new faces and new ways of saying things. The present volume continues this tradition. In the fall of 1997, we sent out a Call for Poems, inviting Michigan poets to submit the best of their recent work. The Call was sent to universities, colleges, and community colleges all over the state and to everyone listed in the Michigan section of the *Directory of American Poets and Fiction Writers.* Several newspapers helped spread the invitation. We defined a contemporary Michigan poet as anyone who has lived in the state at least since January 1995, and any kind of poetry was welcome, published or unpublished. We received 170 submissions, of remarkably high quality. From those, we chose the work of fifty-six poets, being very much aware of all the skillful poems that we were not able to include—and aware that, in any art, judgments are subjective. Though this is only a sampling of the rich ferment of words in the state, readers will find here strong, lively, deeply felt, carefully made poems in a great variety of voices.

The poets in this collection are Michigan residents, writing here in the late 1990s, but most would think of themselves as American writers, not Midwestern or Michigan writers. There are foundries and farms in these poems, trout streams, schoolrooms, restaurants. There are families, friends, lovers—plenty of glimpses of Michigan life. But there's also a taxi driver in Port-au-Prince, live models in the window of a posh boutique in Krakow, fish dying on the third floor at Barneys. These poets have traveled, literally and figuratively. And their recognition has been national as well as regional. Collectively, they have published poems in books and journals issuing from every corner of the country.

"Thank heaven there is no Michigan style," writes Donald Hall in the foreword. We share his gratitude. A reader will find in this collection an exhilarating (or disconcerting) range of styles. For example, consider the variety of narrative voices here. At one extreme, there's the full-tilt storytelling of Murray Jackson's "San Diego Good-Bye," drawing us into the prizefight, the insults, the left hook, and then the redefinition of the speaker's life. Or there's Peter Markus's prose poem, "On Becoming a Bird," told in a leisurely way without embellishment, letting the story of the boy and his father invite us into its strangeness. The talk is clear, natural, matter-of-fact, but what's implied by the father's offering from his lunch bucket--and the son's lowered head, his eating? Other poems, even prose poems, are a lot slipperier, more dreamlike, in their storytelling. At the Interlochen Center for the Arts, according to John Rybicki, "these four kids line up beside four maples and start dragging their bows across each trunk as if sawing them down; as if each tree were a string on a giant cello they were born to play to perfection." And many of these poems, like Laura Kasischke's "My Heart," weave narrative into the fabric of a lyric—a love poem, in this case—moving between present and past, bringing in what didn't happen as well as what did, letting metaphors expand until they become as much a part of the poem as the literal details. That poem ends with a story of childhood magic, a tone about as far from that of Murray Jackson's prizefight as it could get. There is no one Michigan style in this collection, but plenty of Michigan people and places—and a glimpse of the preoccupations and passions that are moving these American poets at the end of the century.

The editors

Priscilla Atkins

Priscilla Atkins (b. 1957) grew up in Illinois. She has lived in Massachusetts, California, Hawaii, and Indiana; since 1994 she has lived in Holland, Michigan, where she is a reference librarian at the Hope College Library. Her work has appeared in journals and anthologies, including *Poetry*, *Tar River Poetry*, the *Cream City Review*, the *Spoon River Poetry Review*, the *Midwest Quarterly*, *Passages North*, and *Sister Stew: Fiction and Poetry by Women*.

The Spanish Professor

We met in the jumble of professorial swagger
gathered around a perennial coffee-tea-muffin table
at the new faculty orientation. It was her height
and long hair, a sweep of arms and hands,
that first caught my attention.
Her short khaki skirt and sleeveless blouse
stood out like crocus sprouts
in a navy blue field. And her legs,
long as runways zooming down to the floor,
shimmered in frosted hosiery, on which
a small, furry green caterpillar was swimming slowly upstream.
It was the perfect match, that leg, and that caterpillar,
as if the two had met through mutual attraction.
And I was torn whether to act on art or etiquette or sheer whim,
when the drone of officialdom sucked me in—
until lunch, when the woman sought me out
and over grapes and melon and innocuous chicken
this Bolivian captain's illegitimate daughter and I
opened like butterflies, floating from past lives,
to love's errors, to what in the hell are we doing here,
our songful chatter unfurling like Rapunzel's hair
that no one dared climb lest they be dropped
into bright-colored fields where a stranger
might reach out and brush your skin,
not to take anything away
but because you are alive and full of wings.

The Boy Who Loved Butterflies

He is in the corner with his book,
his one good hand stroking velvet
colors, the scalloped yellow edge
of a mourning cloak.
Sunlight spills in from the playground,
the clank and clamor of other children.
He has fallen into the silence of wings.
Every morning he falls into them,
the way he fell out of his mother,
into the dark and light,
the dusty blue iridescence
of things only glimpsed once.
He prefers the dorsal view,
the bright-colored fur and jungle-eyed
wings of swallowtails.
He carefully measures beauty
with his flattened palm.
Later, he asks the French teacher
for a new word. "*Papillon,*"
she whispers.
"*Papillon de nuit,* for moth.
Papillons noirs means gloomy thoughts.
If I say, '*Chasse tes papillons noirs,*'
it means you will be happy again."

Gifts from Meiling

Lacquer doors swing open
in the vestibule of a well-tended heart.
The scientist will make a good husband;
he has been asked to go to America.
She gathers threads of sapphire cloth,
simple things to give to strangers,
to slip through her fingers
into the white, white palms of her husband's
boss's wife in Missouri,
where rivers of words slowly erase her history,
shapes of shadows
walking out the door.
Boss's wife brings towels, sheets,
to the university apartment.
Anything else, let her know.
Over the years they exchange many
kindnesses, gaze at each other
from a poignant distance,
a broken bridge, blue veils of air.
Meiling's husband takes a job in Michigan;
still, she remembers the blue of the wife's eyes,
chooses crystal goblets from the shelf at the store.
How carefully she wraps them for their voyage.
Another year, a cashmere sweater, scent
of peach cradled in blue tissue paper, dreams
of rainwater, the blue of ships and railways.
In this town, there is only a river, a Greyhound bus.
She chooses dusk, an embroidered dress,
two bottles of pills.
The silk lining of the dress closing around her,
dark jewel hidden in a stitched bag,
the missing glass slipping
one broken evening in Missouri,
a story a blue-eyed woman passes on.

One of the Last Times I Saw You

For Paul (1956–1993)

The day that I remember was July,
a warm breeze—but not too warm—
coming off the lake.
You were up early, showered and shaved,
crisp as the collar of the business shirt
budding from the edges of your dark suit.
Your hair was a thick swash of India ink.
And your eyes, deep and clear, like they still are
in the photograph from your sister's wedding.

It was a morning like other mornings
when I'd come to visit.
You and I up early, while your lover—my friend—
took his own sweet time getting ready for work.
You ate breakfast out of the refrigerator,
muffin and milk, and then I hugged you
and you were out the door
and down the steep flight of stairs
into the garden.

You took the long way to the front gate.
I watched you bend over lilies and impatiens,
your hand brushing the tops of petals
like the sun on the linden leaves
flapping gently above you.
Through light and shade, you moved
over the flagstones you'd laid
so carefully the summer before.
It was the kind of job you wouldn't do twice.
All that time and labor, and now you slipped over them
and through the gate like a shadow.

On an impulse I ran down the stairs.
By then you were at the corner crossing the street.
I'd come to watch how you moved, to memorize

this pattern of you and sunlight,
of getting up and going to work like any other
beautiful summer day. It didn't have to be
the eighth month after you tested positive
or four months before the IV.
It was a moment a mother would savor:
a healthy son, in the flower of youth,
moving through the membrane of another morning.

Watching for Meteors on Nestucca Bay

I believed I could drink the sun,
and when the last citrus swirls
sank over the horizon
my heart felt small animal tracks
of regret walk down and out of my body
into my older sister's hand.
But darkness was what we'd come for.
My sister said they would be
swift flights of light,
all-of-a-sudden and then gone,
and afterwards you would wonder
whether or not you really saw them.
That night she taught me words
like *cameo* and *swan song.*
I was too young to question so much dust
getting that much attention,
or why people wait in the cold dark,
like any stage-door Johnny,
for a glimpse of greater glory
before it speeds away
in night's long limousine.

Nick Bozanic

Nick Bozanic's most recent book is *This Once: Poems 1976–1996*, from Anhinga Press. He is a winner of the Anhinga Prize for Poetry, a Michigan Creative Artist Grant, and a P.E.N. Syndicated Fiction Award. After nearly twenty years on the faculty at the Interlochen Arts Academy, he is currently teaching at the Punahou School in Honolulu, Hawaii.

Conversion

1

My husband has become a monk, a Mendel
among his bean-rows, a mendicant pilgrim
bowing and scraping on bended knees
to his Jerusalem
artichokes.

Prostrate beneath the sun
and the tomatoes' sacred hearts,
he seeds the earth with his sweat.

Sometimes I think he is mad
with the mysticism of vegetable love—
this exegete of endives,
this cabalist of cabbages.

2

At the kitchen sink, he sets aside
the onions' orbs, the carrots' golden scepters,

and stares strangely down into his filthy palms
spread open as if to hold *The City of God,*

as if he were reading by the light
of the faucet's flow
a scripture only he can see,

as if that soil were a text
in the language of the flesh,

a mystery
of which he does not wish to cleanse himself.

3

After dinner he carries a basket full
of browned lettuce leaves,
beet greens, pea pods, potato peels

out to the edge of the woods
and scatters them there,

sowing the shadows with alms
for the poor who are always with us:
the opossums and the woodchucks and the rabbits and the deer.

4

We make love.
And in the moment of consummation
he lifts himself above me
on arms outstretched like wings,

as if, when most within me,
he were become an angel
born of my body.

5

In the sudden dusk of an August day,
I have seen him genuflect
to the scarecrow's crossed sticks,

a dry wind tearing at its tattered rags.

At Slea Head, County Kerry, Spring

This journey back is a long descent to the shore
and the surf wringing its hands like a widow
in the candle-lit dusk. The wind

scavenges among scant debris, an idler
indifferently fondling and flinging away
whatever it chances on: sapped wrack
or skeletal scraps of wood, spent
crab husks, crow feather, gull feather.

Across night's loam-black barrens,
Orion and his great dog prowl, their prey
scattering in a flight of frightened eyes.

I have traveled a long way to lay my grief to rest
on a crescent of beach beneath this sheer escarpment
facing west across the wastes of sea toward nothing more
than more of night, the unnavigable past. And here

at land's end, in long-sought solitude,
I empty this urn, my heart, pour out its ashes
for the wind to toss on the keening waves.

At first light I'll climb
the cliff-walk up to pastures scoured clean
by the season's hourly shifting sweeps
from snow to sleet to rain to sun.

And where I was,
plover will skitter sidelong
over the silk of wetted sands. Seals,
off shore, will bob and bark in the tidal swirl.

And where I was, the wind will be, fumbling
and vague, like a man who lost so long ago
what he seeks for now, he would not know
if it spoke to him; a man

who has become this moving on, this rummaging
through the litter of what's been left behind.

The Heron

As if he had gathered all his silence into a sack
and bore it with him upon his back,

stoop-shouldered, head bent, in shadowed solitude,
he stalks the river's shallows in the attitude

of one grown weary of the Mind whose coursing depths
he is not made to plumb. He steps

and stills himself, his eyes fixed on the stream
that lisps among the reeds. He seems

older than the Sibyll who from her bottle said
above all else she longed, longed to be dead.

Spinoza, grinding lenses in the Hague,
wore on his face that look, the vague,

distracted look of one who studies hard
to trace upon the Void the lineaments of God.

After experience had taught him that life, lived day-to-day,
amounted to nothing much, he endeavored to assay

if there could be some Good, sufficient in itself,
by which a man might mend his soul from sickness back to health.

And—*mirabile dictu*—he found that Good, or thought he had,
in the communion of Nature and the Mind. Perhaps. The heron's sad

gaze darkens now as the day's light dims.
Soon stars like scintillant fishes school and swim

on the surface of the stream. And still, he stays:
head bowed, devout, the hermit heron preys.

The Mourning Dove

Poor, poor Belle-of-Amherst bird,
poor Emily demure,
who sips the dews of virgin days
and hews, vow-bound, to Vestal ways,

and nests at noon
in the cool wood's shade,
too shy to woo
the sun's immodest praise.

But alone in the night,
she gowns herself
in bridal white
and brushes down
her mouse-brown hair.

The failing candle on the shelf
flutters once in the moonstruck air,
air moved by love to hover near
this barefoot muse whose threnody
attunes all woes to wonder's key.

Her image in the mirror sways
as the candle gutters, the candle dies.
She rises, shuts the window, sighs.
She says, she says
as softly as a kitten's mew,
"So soon, so soon. . . ."

And then a silence,
then a gloom,
as when someone who in the room
was breathing close
has gone, or worse.

Anthony Butts

Anthony Butts was born and raised in Detroit, Michigan. He has earned degrees from Wayne State University, Western Michigan University, and the University of Missouri. His first book of poems, *Fifth Season*, was published by New Issues Press in 1997. His poems have appeared in *Crab Orchard Review, Yemassee, Literature and Belief,* and elsewhere. His work is also included in *Giant Steps: The New Generation of African-American Writers* (edited by Kevin Young and published by William Morrow), and he is included in Rhino Records's new disc of African-American poets, from McKay and Hughes to the present, reading their own work.

Angels

I separate the yellows from the red

crayons broken at the bottom
of a tin container
    having allowed the shafts to chip
in the muggy heat of August.
    Plastic checkers take on flecks
like camouflage in the cabinet
    marked *Saint Leo Elementary*.

There are no children here.

The hallways beneath my feet
are buffed up for the coming semester.
The blanching machines
    have smothered the scuff marks,
trailing down the hall
    with the roar of creation.

I undo the crosses
made of popsicle sticks
and turn the carpets to release
    beetles into the warmth
of the playroom.

It's warm almost like the morning dew
ten years ago at O. W. Holmes Elementary,
moisture weighing down the crickets,
    swings biting—iron against
rusted iron—squealing louder
    as we swing higher into the haze
before first bell. The Braille kids
    drift far out into the fields
to take the swings before noon,
and only physics
keeps them from flying.

Yellow Archipelago

Nebraskan towns float on waves of corn,
Stone harbors strewn with dust instead
Of sand. Women are stranded downtown, on islands

Along the interstate, where sanity is
An addiction. Everyone is normal here.
The diesel and the locust rule the land.

Lights pass like Morse code as freighters
Steam through the night; we evolve from the remnants
Of others, the dream catchers and Mardi Gras

Beads left behind. These women are not
Code breakers, never staying awake
Until the merlot dawn. The night contains

No secrets, the men at the bar endlessly
Speaking into their ears like auctioneers.
Small talk keeps them awake through

The four o'clock hour: the hum the earth makes
The only sound beneath the full moon.
Sex has become a mottled religion. The blue

Molecules of night soak the lawns
As if they'd fallen from the pages of a girl's
Chemistry book. Someday, boys will shoot

Marbles through circles in the dirt.
There's a hole in the middle of the heartland
Where crows sometimes disappear from the tops

Of cornstalks. They resist the pull of gravity
Again, arcing like bloated freighters over
The spurned waves of the archipelago.

A Poe Story

Three a.m. smoke rises from underground
gas lines, the hissing louder than the murmurs
of pigeons, louder than the white winter
clouds passing, heavy with the burden of snow,
nothing released here in Kalamazoo,
neither snow, nor rain, nor any item dropped
from the clenched purse of a woman walking
to her car, footsteps growing louder, quickening
as she spots me walking towards her, towards
the computer center, open twenty-four hours
for people like me, her car between us, gun metal
gray and slush beneath the fenders, the sky
forbidding as my brown face must seem,
her legs making ostrich strides, high heels
scraping the pavement, maybe thinking
my University book bag isn't a knapsack
but a rucksack concealing a gun or knife
bigger than any she's seen in any beefcake
action film where the hero can save a woman like her
from a guy like me, as beautiful as any Poe story,
the spires growing steeper, the icy
smoke of winter puffing faster through her lips, my strides
lengthening like any man who's tried to avoid looking
like a criminal, easing and slowing down as if the indictment
has already been filed, as if suspicion alone
could sentence a man before the crime,
before the thought has entered his mind, before the need
to steal ever took him from the arms of the starving children
he hasn't fathered, or from the woman waving good-bye
to her mother in the window of that first foster care home.

Detroit, City of Straits

February finds a likeness of spring in this unicorn
embossed bedspread. Warm in its closeness, his palm

rests flat against his thigh. Downstairs, the chicken

is frying. The greasy smell wells up through the floorboards
of his small room, a kitchenette for a family cramped

into the upper-half of a one family house from the 30s.

The old stovepipe hole in the roof allows sleet
into a rubber bucket beside his bed

in the only room of the house without heat.

His breath rises on the loose clouds of winter blowing through rags
stuffed between a broken window and its screen.

He dresses quietly in the reservoir of dusk; the time is coming

to run errands for his father, to go looking for the younger brother
running in the streets with those girls from the neighborhood high
    school,

to go and buy a Bible with the money his mother

gave him, to look up those passages
that his pastor dunked him for last week.

Machines

Outside of town, thousands of frogs chortle
And whistle like the frantic sirens and screams
Of an apocalypse, but only the theaters
Are full. Aliens have invaded the earth

Once again. We are never alone, not even
The man who pulls his wife closer in bed
To keep her silent. Her thoughts are like pigeons that crowd
The sidewalks of city parks. The sun rises

Over a misty lake in a starving artist's
Painting. It's the last thing they agreed upon.
Throughout the town, public art stands
At the ready like unnameable metallic

Creatures awaiting a secret message to strike.
A dumpster bears the spray-painted warning:
HEAVEN OR HELL AWAITS YOU as children twirl
Yo-yos with Copernican precision.

A man whispers how machines control
Us all as he watches the toys churn gears.
Pizza delivery vehicles careen
Around corners like the National Guard

On maneuvers. There's a price for being first.
Morning has returned, the sun between
The slats lacing their arms like rubber straps.
Late night static on television gives way

To a commercial involving local store owners,
Toddlers and canines beside them. Families are
Truth. In Hartsburg, children smelly as goats
Or dogs, run through lawns covered with pumpkins.

All is calm, but the festival crowds are days
Away when cars will jam the road through town.
Proclamations will shine like copper doorknobs,
Their closing sentences held together by hinges.

Gladys Cardiff

Gladys Cardiff's poems have appeared in periodicals and anthologies for some twenty years, including such gatherings of Native American poetry as *Carriers of the Dream Wheel, From the Belly of the Shark, Songs from this Earth on Turtle's Back, That's What She Said, Harpers Anthology of Twentieth-Century Native American Poetry,* and *Reinventing the Enemy's Language.* She is an enrolled member of the Eastern Band of Cherokee, and a member of the Native Writers' Circle of the Americas. Her small book, *To Frighten a Storm,* from Copper Canyon Press, won the Washington State Governor's First Book Award in 1976. In 1993, Cardiff moved to Kalamazoo, Michigan, where she recently completed her doctorate in English and Native American studies at Western Michigan University. Her book of poems, *A Bare, Unpainted Table,* was published in 1999 by New Issues Press.

Beautiful Zombies

Kanane'ski Amayehi, Fishing Spider, speaks:

There are things more terrible than death.
To see the turtle tribe swim by,
huge eyes half-dead yet brimmed with tears,
following, always following
some hazy possibility

is to see the manner of my own
predation magnified. Dim-buzz,
punching fang and venom volt,
and all the senses washed away. But theirs
is a communal self-inflicted bite.

As they were once, they were the watery
world's artisans. They studied
the designs of water, the surface tension
of still pools, wind-dapple and deep
whorl of moon-called water.

And as they learned, the patterns grew
upon their bodies so that they and water
seemed one. Their numbers increased, their forays
lengthened. If one was hurt, it thought
into itself the intricacies

of water, and sewed itself back up.
Everyone knows only a turtle
can loosen a turtle's bite. They thought:
"We are living calendars. Time
and we are one. Time heals our wounds."

They no longer studied water. Their bodies
thickened, became deeply
engraved. They slowed down, forgot the trick
of mending themselves. They live a half-
life of perpetual noon. They cast no shadow.

Khv:na

Rustling through the leaves below my window
while I am rising from doughy sleep,
your pip, pip, falling from the eaves,
because it is early light, and nothing much is about
to disturb you—for this little time,
I like you.

I know how you are.
You carry yourself like an only book.

Even the grouse, who had a good voice once,
and who wears forever some of your feathers,
could not teach you how to enter a field
with a beautiful victory cry.
Any noise for you is his drumming.
A door slam, or dog bark, or lawn mower sets you off.
You of the gutturals, the bray,
the nerve-rending screech, go lurching,
silly as a blown cabbage on stake legs
the color of burned bone, driving through the underbrush,
the scalplocks fastened around your neck, bouncing,
bobbling your red wattles,
the jut of your powerful neck, your naked
immune-to-death blue cobbled head,
your talons ripping wet clods and tossing them out behind you.

Gobbler in every sense, a "lord ful fat"
Chaucer would say, "that stemmed as a furnais of lead."

I've seen you snitch the cat's discards,
wagging the small purple lump of bird or mole
crazily through blackberry trailers and foxglove stalks.
A ruckus of gabbling. You swayed over a hen,
the hen going quiet, her neck seized in your beak.
Your bronze feathers cracked and cracked.
Hers glistened and cracked; some fell out
as she sank under the freight of you.
Fan-tail, redness, commotion, quiet.

Khv:na. I am learning to say it.
Khv:na khane:ka. Turkey, he is speaking.
It is too beautiful for you.

Last Days at Petland on Aurora Avenue

Today the signs go up in the window.
As usual, the glass-knife fish, so thin, so shy,
hums with monkish desire
behind the thermometer, his even-tempered brother.
Two matched lines, straight as nails,
living silver and mercury, are floaters
in the corner of the tank, maintaining,
answerable to currents the buried aerator insinuates.
Like a desktop pattern for *50% Off,*
the drowsy water bubbles up
the way bankers do their elusive sums,
their balloons, their inflations, and their obliterating liens.

At the counter, the owner envies the black snake.
He's the smart one, stretched out along the mend
of black electric tape. Why should he care?
The black snakes dreams, unaware, in his cracked tank
of roads that swelter in Baja, of a passel
of black snakes—thousands—throwing up their snouts,
weaving like Arctic seals, bracing each other.
Maybe, if the man at the counter wasn't alone,
he'd do that. They'd do that. Get out. Brace each other.
Braid themselves up like a swami's rope—charmed—zzzzip.

Mom and Pop. That's what I hate. They nod their heads.
The husband and wife are good at courtesy
over the cash receipts, which she takes back
to the small office. He talks to the parrot
and strokes the parrot's cheek. What did the banker,
in her double-breasted suit, call you, Nervous Nellie?
Great Amazon! The bird has been busy,
like some mad typist, pecking the feathers

out of her breast in rows. F! T! K! P!
down to the pebbled flesh. Now stop that, Sweetie,
he croons, or your heart falls out.

We tried, he says. Twelve hours a day, six days a week.
The wife is always in the back.
Not much to tally up, but she keeps at it.
Always busy. Always hopeful. And who can blame her?
I don't. She's embarrassed. Who'd want to stand out here
and man the counter? Nellie, Nellie, I can't remember
which went first, the stock or the customers?
The mice are getting much too big.
The flies buzz up and down their sunlit bin.
Oh, this, this, this, is a sad and dangerous place.

Definition of Space: Giacometti, 1901–1966

> "That is to say, in 1940, the heads became very small, they
> tended to disappear."
>
> from the letters to Matisse

What immensities of space the Greeks knew.
TO fashion those classical busts—that gross massing of clay,
the detail of forehead and cheek . . . *too staggering!*
The attempt would take more than a lifetime.
He's working from models in his grisaille cell, in 1935,
on the Rue Hippolyte-Maindron. The windows, the pans, his hands
are appalled, blue with plaster. His models the same
two women, and his brother, Diego. He is a monk by day.
He prowls at night. One year, two, and then in the Boulevard
Saint-Michel at midnight he watches Isabel walk away
between the rows of houses and lamp posts. *Isabel.*
She turns for a moment, a figure with eyes,
pared down, and yet she remains exactly herself,
even more so, as space encases her, Isabel
rising, holding the void in the strange way
memory recalls a presence. He works from memory.
The figures get smaller. *What terror I felt.* They dream down
to the size of a thumb, each its own pedestal. Knobbed. Eroded.
Impassable space defining the limits a body can bear.
The ribcage, brought to the edge of disintegration,
sometimes crumbling into puffs under his knife. For the heads,
he uses just enough clay to hold them together.
Like the brain really is, he says. *Not one crumb more.*
He flees to Geneva, in 1940. He returns after
the liberation, carrying six matchboxes: three years work.
Now the sculptures get taller. The men walk. The women
stand still, arms against their sides. He pulls
their elbows in. They seem limbless.
Spoons and sockets and a memory of granite.

Michael Delp

Michael Delp lives and teaches in Interlochen. His most recent book is *The Coast of Nowhere: Meditations on Rivers, Lakes and Streams* (Wayne State University Press).

The River Inside

1

Weeks go by, then months, the river iced over. There's no particular place to walk, and each trail to the river is covered again by the time I walk back to the house. Each night before I go to bed I walk to the edge of where I think the bank and the river come together. I lie down with my ear pressed against the ice, listening: This deep vein of water rises north of me, comes down through cedar swamps and meadows, the clear gravel riffles near Grayling. I think to myself on this ten below night that there isn't a voice down there, only an echo. I'm tempted to tell myself I hear things in the current, or sense, in the slow rising of bubbles trapped against ice, that I recognize the message. But there is no message. No voice here in the night coming from the belly of the river. This is the kind of night when anchor ice is born, when the river stiffens. Weeks from now, when the spring rains come, what's left will sweep the river clean, the ice cutting through deadfall, moving rocks for miles downriver. In August, if you're lucky, you can bend down into a pool and find a piece of river shale marked and cut, a kind of sign language left as a reminder that there is no time, no day or week, no month, no full moon, no new moon. Only the slow, constant motion of water and ice, the heave of seasons, the river's long life only getting longer.

2

Back low in the trees the full moon is gathering itself to lift over my head. Upstream the river has the broken castings of moonpath, the dimples of hundreds of tiny fish rising. In the swamp my body turns away from the world, away from roads. I sit under the sweepers of a hundred-year-old cedar, and watch night sift in from the marsh. A nighthawk sluices downriver, the deep "vrooo" of its voice a perfect language for the way the sky and the river switch places. When I stand to speak into the woods I say only my name. I say who I am into the dark and nothing comes back. I wait after each telling and then turn my name into a question. What I hear is only current, the way water deflects from deadfall, a way silence has of catching in the throat. What good comes of this repeated calling, this sending out of my name? This silence? Hours later when I slide into bed, I think I hear something like

I have never heard coming from my lips: a voice like darkness itself, the words rising from my belly, filling the room with something dark and empty as if I were calling back through forty years, my lips alive with whatever it was I had lost.

3

For days now I have come to the river without fishing on my mind, seeking only the way the current takes things away. I drop bits of leaves, pine needles into the river and watch them head downstream. I put my hand in and watch it vanish, then my arm and shoulders and suddenly I am sliding my torso toward bottom, only my head holding in the wash of the Platte. Underwater, my eyes dissolve away, the sun only a memory, the smell of river intensified in whatever it is that I have let myself become. Somewhere downstream under a logjam, under roots, in a bed of gravel, my body comes back to itself, rising up through cool morning air. I carry this sense home: water sifting through rock, through skin, through bone, through memory. Water taking the mind away from itself as if the hands of water could sort and cleanse, and then turn the self loose back into the world. Tonight, walking the hills near the house, I lift my hands to my face and taste the river on my fingers, some small part of me miles away, sidling back and forth in the current, darkness just now settling over the river.

4

Under the bridge I watch the salmon roll and spawn. Later, downstream, I take a drink of death water, my lips falling away. All up and down the river, birds coming in to feed. Inside my chest, my heart thinks it has wings, tries to fly. I speak my own name into the shifting light of an October afternoon, send it out over the water. I speak the names of fish, the birds, all the plants I know. I try to lift off from this place, but my feet won't leave the edge of the river. I squat down near a sandbar and try to memorize the way the rocks have been nudged into place, each stone a marker, a leaving, some way the river has of keeping track of its past. Two old salmon sweep by, their bodies dark and mottled. They move upstream, death riding on their backs. A female rolls toward the male next to her. On the surface of the river I see the reflections of bright maples, and there, in that other world underwater,

I watch them spawn then drift back downriver. I think of how the afternoon gathers itself, how it is that a man can come to the edge of a river and watch death swim by, then go home to make love, or merely look out the window long enough to see himself struggling to get the rider away from his life. And in his sleep he knows the river is moving, the salmon are rolling. Creatures are being ridden to exhaustion.

5

All night I have wandered the woods, headed deeper into the Deadstream. At the river's edge I trace the path of the moon as far upriver as I can see. Mayflies drop out of the air, the surface of the river dimpled with thousands of dying flies. I cast upstream, follow the drift, mending line, always mending. In the semi-dark, in the moonlight, I think I see the outline of my own body as it steps from under the darker arms of cedar sweepers. I stand perfectly still and when it passes directly in front of me, I hear it whisper: "Think of what is left of your life as the water that is passing in front of you right now." I step back on the bank and watch myself trail downriver, then take off my clothes and swim upstream, my mouth gathering in as much water as possible, moonlight, the wash of the river. Wounds I thought I had forgotten suddenly heal, something inside my life gathers itself, turns further inward, lets the river pass through.

6

Today, high clouds being torn apart in the wind. Each time I come home from the river I feel the precipitate of walking upstream, sitting at the smallest of waterfalls where a feeder creek feeds into the Platte. I leave stones there every time, tiny markers, one or two placed in the wash of cold spring water. This afternoon, walking up the drive to get the mail I took a river stone from my pocket, thought of how it was formed by heat and pressure in a time almost before time. Back inside, I put the stone back in the tiny river I have made on top of my desk, each stone perfect, each one a reminder of the message of what was left behind. Tonight, just before I fall asleep, I'll watch this little river like I watch the real one, sure there are fish in every pool, something alive in the trees and deadfall. And when sleep comes I'll carry stones back to the dream river, put them back where they belong.

7

When I wake in the middle of the night I listen for the river, the hiss of rain again, the memory there in the dark of another language I thought I had forgotten. In almost pitch black I hunch down by what's left of the fire, stir the hot ash with a piece of pine kindling. What catches fire comes like a word out of the ground, sifting up through the trees moving slowly away from this place where I have come to forget what I know, forget my own face, my skin, the way I speak. I taste the ashes, carry the voice of embers back to the tent. Before I fall back to sleep I taste the burnt pitch on my tongue. I think of new words for trees, the sky, the way my life has hung in some odd kind of balance all these years. And I think of how the river moves past this camp in the dark, this place where a man is just now struggling to speak something he does not know.

The River Everywhere

FOR CLAUDIA

1

Under the sky, under the bed, under the house, the most beautiful woman I have ever seen is stepping out of her skin, as if out of delicate silk. She holds her skin in her hands as if it were cloth and begins to wring it slowly, and slowly, the most beautiful water begins flowing. When she lifts this water up into this world, her hands cup toward my face and when I drink her, I know for the first time that her river is where I have lived my whole life.

2

Even before I realized it, a river was following me underground. When I slept, it stopped moving and stayed like a shadow under the bed. And when I fished, it coursed, just above bedrock. Once, I remember hearing this river, like a voice from a closet, or a cellar, a place where the husk of a life fell into itself and was saved by the breath of the river.

3

The river is running now over the desk, through my hands, running in the white threads of my shirt, moving in each molecule of my hair. Upstairs I hear my wife and daughter laughing while the current sifts past their bodies. When I go up the stairs they are both resting like stones on the floor, the river running translucent over them, like a second skin.

4

When my daughter falls asleep I hear the river running under her bed, a dream river now and I hear her building a raft in her dream and want to stop her from pushing off. All night I hear her voice calling from downriver, trailing off. I slide toward her mother. Our love is water. I pray to whatever water god would trade the days I have left to turn our lives to water, so that in the instant our lives meet there will be no seam, no difference in the current of her body and the current of mine.

Photo by Robert Wulkowitz

Stuart Dybek

Stuart Dybek teaches in the creative writing program at Western Michigan University. He is the author of a collection of poems, *Brass Knuckles*, and two collections of stories. His poetry, fiction, and essays have appeared in numerous magazines, among them *Poetry, TriQuarterly*, the *Michigan Quarterly Review*, the *New Yorker*, and *Harper's*. He is the recipient of a Michigan Arts Foundation Award, two fellowships from the NEA, a Guggenheim, and an award from the American Academy of Arts and Letters.

Windy City

The garments worn in flying dreams
were fashioned there—
overcoats that swooped like kites,
scarves streaming like vapor trails,
gowns ballooning into spinnakers.

In a city like that one might sail
through life led by a runaway hat.
The young scattered in whatever directions
their wild hair pointed, and gusting
into one another, they fell in love.

At night, wind rippled the saxophones
that hung like windchimes
in pawnshop windows, hooting through
each horn so that the streets seemed haunted
not by nighthawks, but by doves.

Pinwheels whirred from steeples
in place of crosses. At the pinnacles
of public buildings, snagged underclothes—
the only flag—flapped majestically.
And when it came time to disappear

one simply chose a thoroughfare
devoid of memories, raised a collar,
and turned one's back on the wind.
I remember closing my eyes as I stepped
into a swirl of scuttling leaves.

Today, Tonight

Today, wild parakeets awoke
confused to find themselves chattering
in a strange patois.

Today, even the ants are tourists,
and the iguana, camouflaged as a mirror,
has forgotten his true reflection.

The goats must be sorry
they've eaten their passports
because today, like us, they're no longer

sure of who they are or what they're
doing here, otherwise, why else
would goats be swimming out to sea?

⁓

Even the ants are tourists:

they scurry among their ruined pyramids,
toting seeds as if wearing
tiny, white sombreros
a thousand times their weight,

but that's nothing beside the golden weight
of noon—

the heft of light on shoulders,
the enormous shadow
each body tugs along-

so it seems impossible that a red umbrella
opened beside a chrome blue sea
supports the tonnage of a star
descending now too close for comfort

or that an eyelid
can eclipse such radiance.

~

As rising squid knew it would,
a moon that's been hanging around
all day, finally makes its move

and from groves of mango trees
fruit bats unfold their black
umbrellas and hurry to its pull

while a tide ripples through a choir
of mutts on French Town Hill.
Tonight, parakeets retire mimicking

the sputter of sunspots, of dying
frequencies, and citronella candles.
The iguana has assumed

the shape of moonlight.
Are the ants asleep?
Do they dream in unison?

They climb into the starry sky;
by dawn, they've carried off
the Milky Way.

Overhead Fan

Beneath an overhead fan, a man and a woman,
slatted with light leaking through green shutters,
are unaware that they, too, are turning.
The shadow of the blades imparts a slow rotation
to each still object in this hazy room,
and the wobbling fan chirps at its mounting
as if the gecko doing pushups on the mirror
is counting time. Otherwise, it's quiet
but for the whir above the sweaty friction
of their skin. Her mouth gapes
as if emptied of speech; her closed eyes
can't see the shadow that plays
across her eyelids and breasts, and that later
will play across the man's memory.
And though their bodies now press
as if pinned together by centrifugal force,
they feel the spin as if they're hovering—
not like the souls of the newly dead
are said to hover above their abandoned bodies,
but like the hummingbird above the red lips
of the hibiscus just beyond the shutters,
or, high overhead, the black blades
of a frigate bird, centered on extended wings,
above the Gulf Stream's azure gyres.

Inspiration

Finally, down an askew side street
of gingerbread houses held up by paint,
where bony kids crowded around the body
of a cripple who'd been trampled
when the shots rang out,
I spotted a taxi with a raised hood.
The driver was adding motor oil
which was leaking into the gutter

nearly as fast as he was pouring.
I threw in my suitcase and we started
down the mobbed streets,
him laying on the horn, yelling in Creole,
driving, by necessity, with his head
craned out the window. Cracks
ran the length of the windshield
from where the old wound of a bullet
left a crater that vaguely resembled
the shape of a pineapple, and since a cabbie
could never afford to replace the glass,
he'd painted the crater instead—
pineapple yellow with the bullet hole
gleaming at its center like a worm hole
emitting another dimension.
And once he'd painted the pineapple,
wasn't it not only logical, but inspired
to see the cracks that ran from it
as vines, and so he'd painted them
a tangled green that transformed driving
through the streets of Port-au-Prince
into racing blindly through a jungle.
But he wasn't finished yet—
the vines grew flowers: rose red, orchid,
morning-glory blue, and to the flowers
came all manner of butterflies
and newly invented species of small,
colorful birds, twining serpents,
and deep in the shadows,
the mascaraed black-slit, golden eyes
of what may have been a jaguar.

Photo by Bill Olsen

Nancy Eimers

Nancy Eimers is the author of two books of poetry, *Destroying Angel* (Wesleyan, 1991) and *No Moon* (Purdue University Press, 1997). She was the recipient of a Nation/Discovery Award and two NEA Fellowships. Her poems have been published in *Paris Review*, the *Nation, Antioch Review, TriQuarterly, Poetry Northwest, The Best American Poetry, 1996*, and numerous other magazines and anthologies. She teaches in the creative writing program at Western Michigan University and lives in Kalamazoo.

Unplugged

To live inside was the simple first idea behind a house:
a noun
but soft inside. Lined by down.
My husband is playing Nirvana *Unplugged,*
Cobain's wail, stripped down to the wood,
is wood—wild, mad—
akin to the Germanic *Wut,* for "rage."
His "In the Pines" so bare
each unplugged guitar's a door
slammed home.
And then, a little while,
all softnesses that line a human nest
are gone: low voices, the velvet art
of sleeping faces, long breaths to sleep
and the long breaths back again.
Home gone down.
In the pines, in the pines, where the sun don't ever shine.
Jesus, they're fighting again.
Who? I don't know, everybody, everybody.
The woman and man in the song,
my husband and me.
Sometimes,
next door a father shouts at his son, thirteen,
who sobs tightly from the frail shoulders all the way down.
Wood mad. Ready to clobber
his bigger father. *Oh yeah. As if.*
To live inside a tidy box: wasn't that the idea?
I will shiver . . . and the trees have snuck
out of their skeletons again, it's late,
the khaki green of a house across the street
spills from its military square
the whole night through.
In the bluegrass version, Bill Monroe's high whine
mimics the blue-and-gray edges
of wind sawing back and forth in the deepening
graygreen pines;

but Cobain's is all black shriek. An act of erasure.
Someone is rubbing the paper hard . . .
lead bleeds, the paper tears. No color for that.
My girl, my girl, don't lie to me—
a soft black wind
is rubbing out her part in the song. Poor little girl. She has no home.
She has no voice
but the pines.
The common nighthawk lays its eggs on a gravel roof,
no nest—
the killdeer burrows in a cinder bed, its eggs are
spotted, scrawled on, blotched buff-and-black
to look like trash.
I'm going where the cold wind blows.
Who says that?—no one says that
mouthless howl.
Where are we going?
Unplug the lights in the houses,
what becomes of us? Killdeer may even nest in broken glass
between the ties of railroad tracks still in use,
but we—
unplug our houses, and how dark
do we become?
I can hear the neighbor boy still sobbing
madly onto the breast of the family station wagon.

Exam

Had any children? the doctor asks. I say *No*.
And close my lips—the other half of the answer.
If this were a party, I'd feel I had to go on,
even if the other person hadn't asked
Why not? Or *Are you planning on having any?*
They feel free to ask. And almost always, I explain
something about wanting them but not enough,
or how I wish I had two lives: in one of them
I'd have a child by now. But it's no good,
not doing something never sounds as real
as doing it. I seem to stand in for reserve,
my life a keeping back, a state of being
not in active service. But I meant to talk here about time,
the way it passes us at different rates,
two people in the same room—parent and non-parent,
or doctor and patient in an examining room
just big enough for a desk, a table, and a curtain between them,
quite a squeeze with the nurse. For me, the moment has slowed
to simple sentences in present tense.
He asks. I answer. I lie back. She comes in.
They look inside. I answer. No one asked.
For him, the moment probably speeds along,
a paragraph of questions, then another paragraph
of looking with a flashlight. Then
a paragraph of silent writing down.
This doctor doesn't say much with his face.
I'm worried, he's evasive. It's his job
to stay just out of reach.
And crazily, there comes into my head
a job interview I was on once, in a hotel room,
a row of professors sitting on a bed.
One of them smiles and asks me, *Why do* you *think*
so many fiction writers use the present tense these days?
Some answer that the teaching job depends on
hangs in a cloud of thought inside his head.
I can't think, I make something stupid up.

Maybe I should have told him I was terrified
to find myself in that moment, present tense,
stuck in a simple sentence, having to ride it out
by talking and gesturing, hearing my voice in my ears,
which sounds like it doesn't know what it thinks
it's talking about, and my hands move awkwardly
inside the gloves of hands.
I think that man despised the present tense,
and the fiction writers who those days were using it,
despised the short-sightedness of the moment,
any foolish groping in a tiny dark.
I close my eyes and still feel this cold table,
long as my life, and the doctor is gone
except for his gloved hands and the ice-cold
unseen instrument holding me open,
gone the ceiling and walls, just me and the table,
me inside the top half of my clothes,
bra and over it the blouse buttoned up to the top
to keep me safe at home,
and the opening of me between my legs
and the tiny beam of the flashlight
he plays around in me. He's in the dark too,
I guess—he just moves through it faster.
You're probably fine, but let's have an X ray just in case—
make sure nothing sinister's going on.
He smiles a little then, to soften the *sinister*
or maybe just downshifting for an instant
into his natural personality.
As for me, I don't understand anything about time,
how it passes from your parents into you
then into your children, if you have any,
or where it goes to if you don't.
Keep me going, doc, I almost say.
And don't say, but he knows. And God knows what, inwardly, he
    answers.
Then his smile vanishes, it is no longer possible.
He draws the curtain around me,
I put on the bottom half of my clothes,

trying to rustle as little as I can
while, on the other side, he goes and sits down at his desk
and writes, I can *hear* it, another paragraph:
my paragraph. The one I'm rushing through.

Arlington Street

Some lost trumpet blast from Revelations tucked inside the brain
of an aphasiac.
He laughs
as if his tongue were a siren,
as if his teeth were jackhammers.
I've felt the dumptruck of his larynx
churn inside me.
I only know the laugh the way I know the boards in the fence
the laugh comes leaping over every morning, every afternoon,
behind its fence a face
no one has ever seen.
He rambles on that crooked bicycle
of a laugh teetering around a corner, falling off the edge of the joke.
That laugh
of metal stairsteps ending midair, halfway up a burning building,
no way down.
Some days he merely growls
the lower notes of an emery board,
as if the trees and houses on this street
were empty. Mereness. Gold and silver numbers
nailed to shingles,
broken porch swings,
hollow trees.
Some days he makes no sound. As if his mouth were gone.
As if he were the bygone hoot of a derailed commuter train.
As if his mouth were trying to haul the rest of him away.

Photo by Robert Turney

Linda Nemec Foster

Linda Nemec Foster's most recent book *Living in the Fire Nest* (Ridgeway Press, 1996) was nominated for the Small Press Book Award in Poetry and was a finalist for the Nicholas Roerich's Poets Prize. Her poems have been published in numerous journals including the *Georgia Review, Indiana Review, Quarterly West, Nimrod, River Styx,* and *Mid-American Review.* Her work has also been anthologized in *Contemporary Michigan Poetry* (Wayne State University Press), *Catholic Girls* (Penguin/Plume), and *Concert at Chopin's House* (New Rivers Press). She is author of three poetry chapbooks and the winner of two grants for her work from the Michigan Council for the Arts. In 1996 she received a poetry fellowship from the Arts Foundation of Michigan. Most recently, Foster was selected to receive a Literary Achievement Award from the National Writer's Voice Project. The poems included in this anthology are from her new poetry collection, *Amber Necklace from Gdansk,* to be published by Louisiana State University Press.

Amber Necklace From Gdansk

FOR LISEL MUELLER

I don't want the luxury of diamond, luster
of pearl, nor the predictable news of my birth-
stone: emerald, green symbol of love
and success. No sapphires either—no matter
what the ancient Persians said about the blue gem
being responsible for the sky and the ocean.
No jade stone of heaven or picture jasper cave.
I don't want gold or silver, marcasite's northern France.

Give me the prehistoric past that washed ashore
after a storm on the Baltic coast. Fossilized
pine resin that's trapped ancient air. Tears
of the sun that smell like honey, three
strands of the past braided around my neck.
White amber of memory, gold amber of song, dark amber of regret.

Dancing with My Sister

FOR DEBORAH

We're not talking those crazy Polish weddings
in Cleveland, where we both learned how to dance,
clutching each other's sweaty hands, galloping
to the Beer Barrel Polka, and trying not to bump
into Uncle Johnnie and his whirling Chicago Hop.

This is now, tonight, in a smoky bar in Detroit
where two women dancing together can scandalize
any pimp within range. Where the hot-shot
bartender can mix anything and has the wide eyes
to prove it: bloody mary, wallbanger, a zombie
with a spike of lime that will raise the dead.

Above the crowded dance floor, in the maze
of catwalks, the geek of a lighting man
(who reminds us of every boy in high school
who fast-danced with his hands behind his back)
shines the spotlight right on us. And we glow.

Girl, do we glow. Not for the memory of those
distant high school boys whose faces we can't
remember. Not for the fluid desire ebbing
around us on the floor and beyond where silent
men sit in the dark. We glow for the raw truth
of Aretha's voice spelling out RESPECT;
for the way our hair curls down past our shoulders;
for our legs that can out-dance any young thing;
for the miracle that we survived our childhoods—
mother's obsessive cleaning, father's factory shifts,
the Erwin Street mob of pre-juvenile delinquents.
We glow because we came from the same burnt-out dream
of second-generation immigrants and learned to smile
at the closed mouth of loss and dance, dance, dance.

Our Last Day in Krakow

Young woman dressed in total black,
only her face and small hands emerge
from this exile of darkness. She is turned
to the wall in the cloister that surrounds
Wawel Castle. Hands outstretched, eyes
closed, her body swaying in prayer.
Is she Moslem, facing Mecca to the east
where the prophet's Kaaba rises like a die
cast from heaven? Is she Jewish, facing Oswiecim
to the west where Auschwitz and Birkenau
stain the earth: twins of evil catechism,
the serial killer's patron saints?

On the other side of town in the market square,
it's all business—no praying here. Two
live models in the window of a posh boutique:
two trapped beauties imprisoned in blonde,
short black leather, thigh high boots.
Perfectly still for the crowd, for the lone
man who whistles low and wants only
to screw them in front of everybody.

You ask me: what do these women—
the holy and the profane—have in common?
And I reply: the stars and the moon,
the air and the earth, the river and silence,
everything and nothing. How else to explain
the hand of God existing amidst the closing
door of the crematorium, the raw thrust
of the rapist's sole intent? How else
to forgive ourselves for being nothing more,
nothing less than ourselves? Bystanders,
collaborators, hands covered in ash and perfume.

Portrait of My Father, Learning to Count

He is barely two, pale and shy, this boy
who sits at the kitchen table in a house
filled with oak and mahogany, foreign words,
the smell of black bread. He is waiting
for his mother as casually as he waits for the sun
every morning to steal quietly into his room.

She is late, but he sits patiently in this room,
his small fingers play games like those of any boy.
Here's the church, here's the steeple as the day's sun
falls behind the lace curtain. The house
sinks into the sounds of evening: hushed breeze waiting,
holding its breath. Until finally she enters with words

of apology, hushed accents of Silesia. *Janek.* The word
that speaks his name and fills the entire room
like a boundless echo. Her voice repeating it and waiting
for his hesitant reply. And, again, saying the boy's
name as if to convince herself he is here, alive, in a house
in America that not even the wind or rain or sun

in Poland could imagine. How to tell the American sun
"thank you, thank you" when most of the words
she knows are so weighted with syllables the house
starts to forget them. But not the boy in this room.
He will remember because he is the first son, a quiet boy
whose father sweats in a factory, whose mother waits

at the woolen mill for piece work. Their lives waiting
for their son to be something better and not working in sun-
baked fields outside Zielona Gora, a green place the boy
will never see. *Zaden stary, jedyny nowy.* Quietly the words
leave her lips: nothing old, only new. As if the room
could eavesdrop and for a long moment everything does: the house,

damask tablecloth, even the bare trees touching the dark house's
outline. On the table, she places her day's wages and waits
for him to begin. *Jeden, dwa, trzy.* A chant that lifts the room
to heaven. But she doesn't want heaven, only America: its sun-
light, shadow, brick streets, thin dirt. He says the wrong words
again and again until finally he pleases her. The small boy

with his *one, two, three* filling the room. And even the sun
lingers a bit to hear. The house changes with the sound, waits.
One, two, three. Words falling like dusk around her American boy.

Photo by Hank De Leo

Alice Fulton

Alice Fulton's books of poems include *Sensual Math* (W.W. Norton), *Powers of Congress* (David R. Godine), *Palladium* (University of Illinois), and *Dance Script with Electric Ballerina* (University of Illinois, reissue). A collection of essays, *Feeling as a Foreign Language: The Good Strangeness of Poetry*, was published by Graywolf Press in 1999. She has received fellowships from the John D. and Catherine T. MacArthur Foundation, Guggenheim Foundation, and the Ingram Merrill Foundation. Her work has been included in five editions of the *Best American Poetry* series, as well as in the *Best of the Best American Poetry*, edited by Harold Bloom. She is currently a professor of English at the University of Michigan, Ann Arbor.

Call The Mainland

Nature hates a choir. Have you noticed
         the lack of chorus in the country every dawn?
The birds spent the night looking down on earth
       as that opaque, unstarred space.
The vivacious soundscape they create at day
      must be their amazement
that the planet's still in place.

No wait. Time out and whoa. There I go—
coating the birds' tones with emotion,
hearing them as my own. I know, I know.

      Yet I can't say birds aren't feeling
in their hollow bones some resonance of glad
         that night has passed.
     I can't claim their hearts don't shake
when the will to live another day
        in the cascade of all that is
         is strong. Emotion

     makes its presence felt in flesh.
Maybe you've noticed—the body speeds
its reflexes and is moved. It moves. It makes

     the heart, lungs, and gut
       remember their lives
like sleepers between bouts of sleep.
     While more serene delights
are intellect selective, without cardiac effect:
     the mind sparks

at a Borghes story or elegant proof in math,
     a bliss that doesn't shift
        across the blood-
brain barrier. Such heady pleasures
     are never for the birds.
       To be key
rather than bit player, of independent means—

to sound your own agenda in polyphonic overlay
as day take shape==as day takes shape

the birds begin their final take.
They'll never know themselves as symbols
of the sublime. Transcendent
messy shrines, whose music won't stoop
to unison or climax—
tell them I said hi.

Failure

The kings are boring, forever
legislating where the sparkles
in their crowns will be. Regal is easy.
That's why I wear a sinking fragrance
and fall to pieces in plain sight.
I'll do no crying in the rain.
I'll be altruistic, let others relish the spectacle—

as one subject to seizures of perfection
and fragments of success,
who planned to be an all-girl god,
arrives at a flawed foundering,
deposed and covered with the dung
and starspit of what-is,
helpless, stupid, gauche, ouch—

I'll give up walking on water.
I'll make a splash.
Onlookers don't want miracles.
Failure is glamourous.
The crash course needs its crash.

Close

(Joan Mitchell's *White Territory*)

To take it further would mean dismantling doorframes,
so they unpacked the painting's cool chromatics
where it stood, shrouded in gray tarpaulin
near a stairwell in a space so tight
I couldn't get away from it.
I could see only parts of the whole,
I was so close.

I was almost in the painting,
a yin-driven, frost-driven thing
of mineral tints
in the museum's vinegar light.
To get any distance, the canvas or I
would have to fall down the stairs
or dissolve through a wall.
It put me in mind of winter,

a yin-driven enigma and thought
made frost. When I doused the fluorescents
it only became brighter.
The background spoke up
in bitter lungs of bruise and eucharist.
Of subspectrum—
a sentence left unfinished because
everyone knows what's meant.

It was a home for those who don't go out
for sports: the closeted, oddball, marginal
artists in the storage of the world's indifference,
whatever winters await us next.
I was almost in its reticence

of night window and dry ice, its meadow
lyric barbed in gold, almost
in the gem residence
where oils bristle into facets

seen only in the original, invisible in
the plate or slide
since a painting is not an illustration
but a levitation dense
as mind. As this minute
inheriting its history along innumerable lines.

==The enigma is so diligent==
I miss it when I visit it==

It shrinks to *winsome* in a book.
Its surface flattens to sleek.
In person, it looked a little dirty.
I could see the artist's hairs
in the pigment—traces of her
head or dog or brush.

==I stood too close==I saw too much==

I tried to take the long view
but there was no room.
I saw how turpentine had lifted the skin,
leaving a ring, how the wet was kept
on the trajectories, the gooey gobs of
process painted in. Saw dripping
made fixed and nerves and
varicosities visible.
I saw she used a bit of knife
and left some gesso showing through,
a home for lessness that—
think of anorexia—
is a form of excess.

While painting, she could get no farther away
than arm's length.
While seeing parts of the whole,
she let the indigenous breathe
and leave a note.

She dismantled ground and figure
till the fathoms were ambiguous—
a sentence left unfinished
because everyone knows what's meant,
which only happens between friends.
The lack of that empathy embitters,
let me tell me.

==I miss you when I visit you==
I stand too close==I see too much==

You put me in mind of winter where I live,
a winter so big I'll have to dismantle myself
to admit it: the always winter
and its consolations of flint.
This is not an illustration.
It's what I saw when the airbag opened,
slamming me with whiteness like the other side.
I came to consciousness on braced arms,
pushing my face from the floor
in order to breathe,
an arm's length from unbeing, as it seems.
I was what flashed through me

in full frost. We were life to life,
in our flesh envelopes,
insubstantial, air to air and you and I.
Though we could see only parts of the whole,
we felt its tropism.
We leaned toward, liked,
its bitter lungs. We almost were that
winter tissue and cranial-colored paint.
We were almost in the picture. We were close.
We left each other a note.

Mary Jo Firth Gillett

Mary Jo Firth Gillett was born in Lansing, Michigan, and has lived in the Detroit area most of her life. Her poems have appeared in the *Michigan Quarterly Review, Harvard Review, Green Mountains Review, Sycamore Review, Crab Orchard Review, Third Coast, Passages North, Poetry Northwest, Nimrod*, and other journals. She is winner of the 1998 Detroit Writer's Voice Chapbook Contest, the 1999 Select Poets Series chapbook competition, and the New York Open Voice Poetry Competition.

Word

Not just a syllable, a ululation, click, roll, slur, trill. I want
the whole damn thing, the roller-coaster ride of consonant, vowel,
accent and innuendo. I want serendipity do-da, I want somnambulant
rapture, and I want it mal, bad—malcontented, maladjusted,
    maloccluded.
I want it alpha and penultimate—there is no end. I want the sound
and everything it conjures up, the surprise—that wasp nest
still clinging to the eaves of memory, thin paper that seems empty
but buzzes to life with a little warming—or should I say warning—
a little onomatopoeic poltergeist in my head, a haunting, a mesh
of sound and moment, fit tight as tiles in a Moroccan mosaic,
or the cowry shell wrapped about its softer insides, the subtle
pianissimo of what it is—these sounds our companions, linking us
one to another like some species specific duet—or should I say
diet—the panda and its bamboo, the koala and its eucalyptus, how
things are joined as, when I say a word—veranda, for example—
or a name, Einstein—it never means strictly what I want it to
because of the baggage, everything it ever was—including the
    madness—
everything the seine net of memory can hold—squirming shiners,
bits of vegetation, muck and grit and algae—the small, the smell of it,
so that even now, dry and propped against the garage, this net teems,
the wind catching at its webbing, the primal smell like bedsheets
after sex—a skin, a skein of sound, whirl of x and y, both cargo
and carriage—like any word—part cure, part tremor at the core.

Spindrift

What hasn't already been said about
the moon, the stars? And though, Love,
we are no heavenly bodies, no constellations,
in our eyes there still lingers the light—somehow—
of a collapsing star, light too dim to pierce
these onion days. But see how the very world
works for us, nothing wasted, nothing lost—
each tear that slips to the anonymity of collar
or floor, each molecule of rain that seeps
to alligator sewers—I've read—once coursed the points
of pyramids, knew the likes of Cleopatra, and
after a season of spindrift or snow will
melt again to hot sands, thirst that is
sudden artesian and slow Paleozoic,
tiger's teeth and trilobite's scuttle across salt seas,
both larger than the sky's red giant,
smaller than the radium atom emitting its lethal dose
to Madame Curie. In this time, both briefer
than the engineer's nanosecond and longer,
much longer than the 100 million years
it has taken us to get to this moment, stripped
of its coverlet weight, I marvel at our bodies—
each other's bookmark—keeping alive the passage
called passion, the red quickening pulse that,
like the ratchet sound of a child's wind-up toy,
like the edge of the evaporating puddle,
fades only reluctantly as each cell whispers,
I am here. You are here. It matters.

Memory

is the empty sock on the floor that still holds
the shape of the foot. It's a thin strip
of the entire picture, shredded by the eyes'
sense of event, the mind like Dan Rather on location—
on the moon—a place with comparatively little
gravity, yet cliched and thus, like Swiss cheese,
full of holes. This business of thinking back
to a point in time is like writing a poem that
cites another poem—Dobyns does it—a man
explains to his wife that the Stevens line,
Let be be finale of seem, means *what exists is
more important than what seems to exist.*
Just goes to show how difficult it is to explain
the essentially evocative. What I want to do
is up the ante—write a poem that quotes a poem
that quotes a poem. Because that's exactly
the problem with memory. It's like those nesting
matryoshka dolls, the features of the smallest
so diminutive who knows what they really look like?
Just a semblance of the real—like Mount Rushmore—
not really flesh, but hard and craggy, and much
much bigger than real life, and bigger is better,
right? The problem is that truth—read that memory—
is always in tension with a soluble fish. Yes,
like Simic, I believe in it—flux, not finale—
everything on the edge of becoming, ready
to slip into something else—not like
dolls inside dolls inside dolls but children
holding a flashlight under a colander,
casting stars into a darkened room—each moment,
each breath, air in a windsock, spilling out.

World Enough

Whether I chalk it up to Newtonian physics
or just some impulse driven by the first whip
of a flagellating cell, I'm in it for the duration,
time and motion until the stop sign, and even then
the body's slow sinking into itself like fallen fruit.
I'm not talking about apples here—there is no moral—
only movement micro/macrocosmic, bodies mechanical
and protoplasmic, and how I watch the watch movement—
tick, tick—as if it's a tiny cosmic system, a study
in time and space—what else but continuum—because
God knows I want it quantifiable, a sort of
temporal hieroglyphic minute-to-minute record,
history of the path taken or not—tick, tick—my own
personal time bomb as we plunge through space and
each other, our bodies, if you believe quantum physics—
like the rest of the world—mostly made up of
space. In the midst of the falling, skydivers
aiming for a small plot of ground—"X" on the zoo map,
"G" in the woman's body, arrow pointing "You are here"—
I see it's a package deal, flesh and place—and
aren't we what we've always been—rhythm and matter
composed in treble and bass, songbird's trill
and Beethoven's da-da-da-DUM pressing into the shell
of the ear, a golden hum, cider sloshing
the sides of the jug. How I drink it in, a con
on death row looking for reprieve, the thub-dub behind
my bars quickening because, in this world of dung beetle
and rhinoplasty—tick, tick—it is all so wonderfully
with me I have to ask—who could willingly give it up?

In the spectrum of light,

in this space all around us, what the dictionary calls
the three-dimensional field of everyday experience,

in the humid stalls of Singapore where the dark translucence
of hundred-year-old eggs is created in just ninety days,

in the quirky dairy town of Mooers, New York, town of
Holsteins and milking machines (*Welcome to Mooers!* the sign says),

something else is felt. The wings of the dragonfly, life span
48 days, dart through it. My daughter feels the urgency

as she broods over the drooping bean plants of her science project.
It will not help her to know that the elephant can live 70 years

in captivity. Though the life expectancy of a chipmunk is 1.3 years,
a beetle 21 days, a butterfly two weeks, these numbers do not console
    me.

There must be some iridescence to salvage, something
of what floats like soap bubbles, puffs of breath

in the rooms we live. Did that one work, the metaphor?
I do keep fishing for a real keeper, a taxidermist's delight

I can nail to the wall, a plaque to preserve, to lure me
just below the surface to warm currents where I can almost feel

The Roy G Biv of sunlight on scale. I need some reliquary proof—
a surface to finger, a trace, a trail, a shell I can put to the ear.

I work at it—like the Incas who had no system of writing,
only the quipu, a complex of knotted strings

which recorded statistics and the sequence of stories,
the details lost in the knots.

Photo by Philip T. Dattilo

Linda Gregerson

Linda Gregerson is the author of *The Woman Who Died in Her Sleep* (Houghton Mifflin) and *Fire in the Conservatory* (Dragon Gate), as well as a book of criticism, *The Reformation of the Subject: Spenser, Milton, and the English Protestant Epic* (Cambridge University Press). Her awards include the Levinson Prize from *Poetry* magazine, the Consuelo Ford Award from the Poetry Society of America, and grants and fellowships from the National Humanities Center, the Arts Foundation of Michigan, and the National Endowment for the Arts. Gregerson directs the MFA program in creative writing at the University of Michigan, where she also teaches Renaissance literature. She lives in Ann Arbor with her husband and two daughters.

For the Taking

And always, the damp blond curls,
        on her temples
    and bountifully down to her shoulder blades,

the rich loose curls all summer mixed with sand
        and sweat,
    and the rare, voluptuous double

curve of her nether lip—most children lose
        that ripeness before
    they can talk—and the solemn forehead,

which betokens thought and, alas
        for her, o-
    bedience, and the pure, unmuddied line

of the jaw, and the peeling brown shoulders—
        she was always
    a child of the sun . . . This

was his sweet piece of luck, his
        find,
    his renewable turn-on,

and my brown and golden sister at eight-
        and-a-half
    took to hating her body and cried

in her bath, and this was years,
        my bad uncle did it
    for years, in the back of the car,

in the basement where he kept his guns,
        and we
    who could have saved her, who knew

what it was in the best of times
              to cross
        the bridge of shame, from the body un-

encumbered to the body on the
              block,
        we would be somewhere mowing the lawn

or basting the spareribs right
              outside, and—how
        many times have you heard this?—we

were deaf and blind
              and have
        ever since required of her that she

take care of us, and she has,
              and here's
        the worst, she does it for love.

from *The Woman Who Died in Her Sleep*

2

When Megan chose the fifteenth-century sculpture
              rooms, I
        realized with some chagrin

she hadn't any notion who these
              people
        were. The one in blue,

I said, is Mary, and the one
              she's
        holding in her lap . . . till Megan

got the gist of it. And here,
              I said,
        is how you'll know him when they take

him down: five wounds. But my five-
             year-old
         daughter saw six. Have I

told you—do you know for yourself—how the
             sweetness
         of creation may be summed up in the lightfall

on a young girl's cheek? The wound
             she hadn't yet
         learned to ignore, the mortal one, was where

the child had once been joined
             to something else.

Fish Dying on the Third Floor at Barneys

The clothes are black and unstructured this fall,
             enlivened
         here and there by what appears to be monastic

chic: a crucifix of vaguely Eastern prov-
             enance,
         a cowl. My friend, fresh out of drama school,

explains to me how starkly medieval woolens
             were cut:
         few seams, to spare unraveling, the neck-

notch centered in a single length of cloth.
             High season,
         maiden season at the uptown store, austerity's

a kind of riff in suede and silk. Sumptuous
             charcoals,
         lampblack, slate. And lest the understatement

lose its edge, glaziers have installed
        these fine
    aquaria, within whose bounds, superbly

not for sale, not just at present, swim
        the glories
    of a warmer world. The sun

was always a spendthrift, wasn't it?
        —cadmium
    yellow, electric blue, and lines that parse

as eat-your-heart-out. Nature's own
        extravagance,
    and functional, in fins and tails.

But something's wrong. The angelfish
        near gloves
    and belts is on its side and stalled, grotesquely

heaving at the gills. Says the
        shopper
    to her boyfriend, "What's it *doing?*"

and she's horrified. Frank
        dying
    makes a fearful sign of life in here,

it puts the people off their food.
        Your mother,
    said my father when I teased

her once, and nastily, Your mother always
        liked
    to save. And who should know

but he and I, who'd lived on her prevenient
            thrift?
        He didn't say, Uncluttered

is the privilege of the rich these days.
            Or: In
        a world of built-in obsolescence, saved

means saddled with. He said much later,
            This
        (I held his hand) This is a bad

business. Nailbeds blue, blue
            ankles,
        dusky ears. His mucus-

laden lungs and their ungodly labor.
            Father,
        while there's air to breathe, I mean

to mend my manners.

Robert Haight

Robert Haight (b. 1955) lives at Hemlock Lake in Cass County and teaches writing at Kalamazoo Valley Community College. A poet and essayist, he has published in a wide variety of periodicals, including the *Northern Review, Oxford Magazine,* the *Rockhurst Review,* the *South Coast Poetry Journal,* and others, and has published a chapbook of poetry, *Water Music.*

Issa Casts a Dry Fly at the Moon

A white stone in moonlight
as black curls of water
shadow its edges
and pass downstream
into the further darknesses
under the pine trees

he wears a purple gown
the color of night sky
and casts a strand of spider web
at the moon
floating on the river

for a trout
whose skin is empty space
and whose scales are stars
to take this fly
he has spun from the thin air
of his breath

so he can see the moon shatter
and watch the river's swift hands
ease the pieces together
into one moon again

as if there were no trout
hiding under the moon
whispering *current, current, current.*

This River

This is the river
that didn't appear on the map

that spread across the end
of one of those endless two-tracks
angling off a logging road

or, perhaps, it wasn't a two-track
at all, just a space between the trees
that you mistook and ended here.

No tracks but the curve
of deer hooves in the bank sand,
the path of ancients
disappearing into brush.

The river surges by,
its unmistakable clarity.
Even in the pines
on the far bank, each needle
sparks a single fire
rubbed from it by the wind.

Fish Flies

Fish flies filled that June night, drawn from the lake to the lights along shore, clouds boiling in the halo of every street light. Fish flies covered each brick on the houses, curtained the windows of the storefronts, coated the screens. We were sixteen, driving around in the glow of dashlights behind a cloud of smoke we passed from hand to hand. We circled the courts back to Lakeshore Road, the odometer spinning miles out of nothing but some urgency to glimpse the bodies of the girls we desired, silhouetted by translucent wings on the twitching panes of their bedroom window. We listened to the low drone of a Seger tape, the fish flies crackling like static under the tires. In the morning the shopkeepers would sweep piles off the sidewalks with a push broom. We would hear of a few cars that slid out of control where fish flies had packed into a thin layer like ice. We didn't know then they survived for years in the shallow mud until the night they shed their skins and flew in search of a mate. We thought they only lived for one day, pulled the smell of lake water over the night, over us, and left it there.

Two Dogs with Children

Say you've just come over the hump
and can see one dog on the side of the highway,
ribbons of blood and drool flagging
from its mouth, trickling
off the shoulder into rust stained dirt.
It is the dog that has chased your car
each morning on your way to work,
made you brake as it trotted
ahead of your left front tire,
until far enough from home it turned
away and you could accelerate to sixty-five.
Four kids stand around
where their front yard meets the road.
It is their dog but they haven't moved it.
They are trying to kill time,
waiting for someone to get home.
You crawl past them, see their eyes turn
to where their dog fixes
its stare into a tiny galaxy of asphalt,
while their other dog keeps its distance,
its long coat slapped to life
from a stream of wind by the barn.
None of it helps.
The next Monday they wait
for the school bus and watch
the other dog become the first,
tearing after each truck and car cruising by,
snarling at the bus tires.
Each morning you pass
the dog is still alive,
crouched to jump in front of your car
while the children look down, embarrassed,
perhaps as much of their bright nylon coats
and rubber boots or the junk busses
and rusted sixties pickups
rotting in the weeds that make their yard

as any training they owe their dog.
And so I ask what do you do?
Do you stop and shout at them
to get that goddamn dog off the road,
to tie it to a chain and when it starts
after the wheels to yank it back until it learns?
Or do you take them in your arms
and whisper while you touch their hair
that one dog already has been crushed
before their eyes?
Or do you just drive ahead,
accelerate into your life,
where leash laws and agencies
promise all the necessary repairs?

Photo by Dennis Gripentrog

Jim Harrison

Jim Harrison is a poet and novelist who lives in northern Michigan, the Upper Peninsula, and on the Mexican border.

from *Geo-Bestiary*

1

I can hear the cow dogs sleeping
in the dust, the windmill's
creak above thirty-three
sets of shrill mating birds.
The vultures fly above the corrals
so softly the air ignores them.
In all of the eons, past and future,
not one day clones itself.

2

I walked the same circular path today
in the creek bottom three times.
The first: a blur, roar of snowmelt
in creek, brain jumbling like the rolling
of river stones I watched carefully
with swim goggles long ago, hearing
the stones clack, click, and slow shuffle
along the gravel.
The second time: the creek is muddy,
a Mexican Jay follows me at a polite
distance, the mind slows to the color
of wet, beige grass, a large raindrop
hits the bridge of my nose, the remote
mountain canyon has a fresh dusting
of snow. My head hurts pleasantly.
The third time: my life depends
on the three million two hundred seventy seven
thousand three hundred and thirty three
pebbles locked into the ground so I
don't fall through the thin skin of earth
on which there's a large coyote turd full
of Manzanita berries I stepped over twice
without noticing it, a piece of ancient chert,
a fragment of snakeskin, an owl eye
staring from a hole in an Emory oak,
the filaments of eternity hanging in the earthly

air like the frailest of beacons seen
from a ship mortally far out in the sea.

7

O that girl, only young men
dare to look at her directly
while I manage the most sidelong of glances:
olive skinned with a Modigliani throat,
lustrous obsidian hair, the narrowest
of waists and high French bottom, ample
breasts she tries to hide in a loose blouse.
Though Latino her profile is from a Babylonian
frieze and when she walks her small white dog
with brown spots she fairly floats along,
looking neither left or right, meeting no one's
glance as if beauty was a curse. In the grocery
store when I drew close her scent was jacaranda,
the tropical flower that makes no excuses.
This geezer's heart swells stupidly to the dampish
promise. I walk too often in the cold shadow
of the mountain wall up the arroyo behind the house.
Empty pages are dry ice, numbing the hands and heart.
If I weep I do so in the shower so that no one,
not even I, can tell. To see her is to feel
time's cold machete against my grizzled neck,
puzzled that again beauty has found her home in threat.

8

Many a sharp-eyed pilot has noticed
while flying in late October
that remnant hummingbirds rob piggy-back
rides on the backs of southward flying geese.

10

I know a private mountain range with a big bowl in its center that you
find by following the narrowest creekbed, sometimes crawling until you
struggle through a thicket until you reach two large cupped hands of
stone in the middle of which is a hill, a promontory, which would be
called a mountain back home. There is iron in this hill and it sucks

down summer lightning, thousands and thousands of strokes through time, shattering the gigantic top into a field of undramatic crystals that would bring a buck a piece at a rock show. I was here in a dark time and stood there and said, "I have put my poem in order on the threshold of my tongue," quoting someone from long, long ago, then got the hell off the mountain due to tremors of undetermined source. Later that night sleeping under an oak a swarm of elf owls (*Micrathene whitneyi*) descended to a half-dozen feet above my head and a thousand white sycamores undulated in the full moon, obviously the living souls of lightning strokes upside down along the arroyo bed. A modern man, I do not make undue connections though my heart wrenches daily against the unknowable, almighty throb and heave of the universe against my skin that sings a song for which we haven't quite found the words.

12

I was hoping to travel the world
backwards in my red wagon,
one knee in, the other foot pushing.
I was going to see the sights I'd imagined:
Spanish buildings, trellised with flowers,
a thousand Rapunzels brushing their long
black hair with street vendors singing
the lyrics of Lorca. I'd be towed
by a stray Miura over the green Pyrenees,
turning the bull loose before French customs.
At the edge of the forest René Char was roasting
a leg of lamb over a wood fire. We shared
a gallon of wine while mignonettes frolicked for us.
This all occurred to me forty-two
years ago while hoeing corn and it's time
for it all to come to pass along with my canoe
trip through Paris, with Jean Moreau trailing
a hand in the crystalline Seine, reading me Robert Desnos.
Why shouldn't this happen? I have to rid
myself of this last land mine, the unlived life.

16

My favorite stump straddles a gully a dozen
miles from any human habitation.
My eschatology includes scats, animal poop,
scatology so that when I nestle under this stump
out of the rain I see the scats of bear, bobcat,
coyote. I won't say that I feel at home
under this vast white pine stump, the roots
spread around me so large in places your arms
can't encircle them, as if you were under the body
of a mythic spider, the thunder ratcheting
the sky so that the earth hums beneath you.

19

I sat on a log fallen over a river and heard
that like people each stretch had a different voice
varying with the current, the nature
of its bed and banks, log jams, boulders,
alder or cedar branches, low slung
and sweeping the current, the hush of eddies.
In a deep pool I saw the traces of last night's moon.

26

In Montana the badger looks at me in fear
and buries himself where he stood
in the soft sandy gravel
only moments ago. I have to think
it's almost like our own deaths
assuming we had the wit to save money
by digging our own graves or gathering
the wood for the funeral pyre.
But then the badger does it to stay alive, carrying
his thicket, his secret room in his powerful claws.

28

The wallet is as big as earth
and we snuffle, snorkel, lip lap
at money's rankest genitals,
buried there as money gophers, money worms,

hibernate our lives away with heads
well up money's asshole, eating, drinking,
sleeping there in money's shitty dark.
That's money, folks, the perverse love
thereof, as if we swam carrying an anchor
or the blinders my grandpa's horses wore
so that while ploughing they wouldn't notice
anything but the furrow ahead, not certainly
the infinitely circular horizon of earth.
Not the money for food and bed but the endless
brown beyond that. I'm even saving
up for my past, by god, healing the twelve hour
days in the fields or laying actual concrete blocks.
The present passes too quickly to notice
and I've never had a grip on the future,
even as an idea. As a Pleistocene dunce
I want my wife and children to be safe
in the past, and then I'll look up from my money
fucking grubbing work to watch the evening
shadows fleeing across the green field next door,
tethered to these shadows dragging toward night.

34

Not how many different birds I've seen
but how many have seen me,
letting the event go unremarked
except for the quietest sense of malevolence,
dead quiet, then restarting their lives
after fear, not with song which is reserved
for lovers, but the harsh and quizzical
chatter with which we all get by:
but if she or he passes by and the need
is felt we hear the music that transcends all fear,
and sometimes the simpler songs that greet sunrise,
rain or twilight. Here I am.
They sing what and where they are.

Photo by Robert Turney

Bob Hicok

Bob Hicok's *Plus Shipping* was published by BOA Editions in 1998. *The Legend of Light* won the 1995 Felix Pollak Prize and was an ALA Notable Book of the Year. His poems have been included in *Best American Poetry* 1997 and 1999, and in the *Pushcart Prize XXIV*. An NEA Fellow for 1999, he also has poems coming out in the anthologies *9MM: Poets Respond to Violence in America* and *American Diaspora: Poetry of Exile.*

Building a Painting a Home

If I built a barn I'd build it right into the sky

with windows twice as large as walls and ringed
with theoretical pines, clumps of green on simple sticks

and doors cut from the ocean, doors that wave
and doors that foam and shadows inside to eat

every cow I own because I'm afraid of cows,
two stomachs imply that aliens are involved,

moo is what the brain-washed say, my fields
would be green until yellow and yellow

until white, acres of albino wheat
for the manufacture of weightless bread,

I only eat what floats in a house that spins
as the weather vane turns, a house that follows

a rooster in love with wind, the sky
and my barn are blue and the sky also floats,

there's nothing to hold anything down,
even eternity's loose and roams the erotic

contortions of space, even my children
recognize tomorrow better than they remember

today, if I built a barn I'd build the land
and the sun before that, I'd spread the canvas flat

with my hands and nail it to the dirt, I'd paint
exactly what I see and then paint

over that until by accident something habitable
appears, until the kettle screams on the stove,

until the steam is green and the sound is gold.

Plus Shipping

"Inspired by Kokopelli, Golfer-Pelli is a fun-loving symbol
for our times."

from one of the 400 mail-order catalogs we received last
year

Certainly it was a premonition of a Navajo warrior that men
in plaid would take up sticks and club a ball into a hole's

submission. And that a god of prosperity and joy, flute
player, source of the wind's conversational obsessions,

secretly longed to represent the beef-fatted, tax-sheltered,
divot-spewing tribe in their hunger for real estate

made green and blemish free, acres of fertilized eternity.
It happened like this: someone named Stan or Rita

spanked their cell-phone open in Manhattan traffic, called
Lou Ellen or Robbie and went on at an ecstatic pitch

about a program they saw on the Learning Channel last night
that documented cave paintings in Arizona of this guy

with hair like spiders and a body twisted as if
he'd swallowed a hurricane, and wouldn't it make a hot

knick-knack if we put him in knickers with a seven-iron
in his hands? And later, after the market research,

after paying one company to come up with a name, another
to design the eyes, hips, the casual-yet-indigenous-gestalt

needed to represent a sport built around the prophecy
of leisure, Stan or Rita will confess to something like

inspiration, a little zing, a small frisson disrupting
their preoccupation with fear that screamed low

cost, high profit. And I wouldn't mind if I were ten
or drunk most of the time, if I'd missed

even half the commercials utilizing the dramatic skills
of Super Bowl quarterbacks, the winks of senators

who reached for president but fell one scandal short,
wouldn't care if I could forget Michael Jackson

trying to sell his crotch, Elizabeth Taylor
hustling the diamonds of her scent, if just once

someone would stand before a camera and simply say
I've made this offensive thing but won't leave you alone

until you send me ten bucks. Golfer-Pelli's destined
for mantles, to fill that hole between vase and clock

where space bleeds, needing the bandage of artifact.
And what of the Buddha alarm clock, Shiva spice rack,

the shoe polisher in which red and green fuzzy wheels
pop from Mohammed's ears and spin your leather clean?

Give it time and you'll get your crack at each
and more, for as we eat and sleep there's someone

flipping through a magazine, strolling the open veins
of ruins, touching forgotten texts, sculpted faces

of a people centuries gone, who can't help but think
there's beauty and sorrow and money in every one of these.

Other Lives and Dimensions and
Finally a Love Poem

My left hand will live longer than my right. The rivers
    of my palms tell me so.
Never argue with rivers. Never expect your lives to finish
      at the same time. I think
praying, I think clapping is how hands mourn. I think
    staying up and waiting
for paintings to sigh is science. In another dimension this
      is exactly what's happening,

it's what they write grants about: the chromodynamics
    of mournful Whistlers,
the audible sorrow and beta decay of *Old Battersea Bridge.*
      I like the idea of different

theres and elsewheres, an Idaho known for bluegrass,
    a Bronx where people talk
like violets smell. Perhaps I am somewhere patient, somehow
      kind, perhaps in the nook

of a cousin universe I've never defiled or betrayed
    anyone. Here I have
two hands and they are vanishing, the hollow of your back
      to rest my cheek against,

your voice and little else but my assiduous fear to cherish.
    My hands are webbed
like the wind-torn work of a spider, like they squeezed
      something in the womb

but couldn't hang on. One of those other worlds
    or a life I felt
passing through mine, or the ocean inside my mother's belly
      she had to scream out.

Here, when I say *I never want to be without you,*
    somewhere else I am saying
I never want to be without you again. And when I touch you
      in each of the places we meet,

in all of the lives we are, it's with hands that are dying
    and resurrected.
When I don't touch you it's a mistake in any life,
        in each place and forever.

Finally I Buy X-Ray Glasses

At 13 I questioned when it would stop, this
seeing through. Wouldn't my supercharged glance
invade walls and blouses and bones, pierce
to atoms and smaller still, even pass
through the film of the soul as it tunneled
to the scowling mask of God, leaving me blind
for the sin of snooping flesh? I was a literalist
who believed secrets were solved inside, that
any mystery, even lust, could be taken apart,
pieces sifted down to the blessing of the whole.
That was before the burn of your face at dusk
across the wooden table, something more
than your body in the moment's text, light
turned to skin, to words that circled the room
like the shadows of birds: before you moved
from dresser to bed, your flesh a vestige
of candlelight, every need, all love borne
to the surface, a radiance I could touch.
Last night I came home to a box
from the Johnson Smith Company, X-Ray Specs
and arcana describing how to keep
their Zeus-power in check. What began
as a laugh became kisses that chased us
into bed. You wore the glasses,
I closed my eyes and felt you
                                watching me
thinking of you
                    looking through me
as I stared back, which is exactly
what making love should be like.

Photo © 1998 Anthony James Dugal

Conrad Hilberry

Conrad Hilberry grew up in Ferndale and has taught at Kalamazoo College for many years. His most recent books are *Sorting the Smoke: New and Selected Poems* (University of Iowa Press, 1990) and *Player Piano* (Louisiana State University Press, 1999). *Taking Notes,* a chapbook of animal poems, was published by Snowy Egret in 1999.

The Expatriates

Here in the sun, the long December days
defy sadness. Courtyards, narrow streets,
walls still warm at evening. And flowers—
geraniums, conchas, the bleeding fuchsias—
each with its own faint smell, incense settling
on the cobblestones. The bent arms
of bougainvillaea are tricked out in crimson
or magenta. In the north, we remember,
our grief had reasons: confinement and cold,
the pipes frozen, new snow so deep you wake,
look out, and sink back into the week-long
loneliness. But here on this high plateau,
the air is thin, the clouds thin, the days
attenuated, beaten like gold until
they stretch unbroken from horizon to
horizon. At long distance we hear our children
speaking about their lives. "Really," we say,
"how are you?" "Oh, thanks, I'm all right," sadness,
a voice traveling two thousand miles over
desert and dry riverbed, thinning down
to a single fiber—as in the garden
the orchids lay their small mouths on the neck
of the evening, as grackles scream into the pruned
trees, as lemon tea steeps in the pot
on the wrought-iron table and we talk
of conveniences and inconveniences.
Far away, a dog howls as though
the enchilada woman splashed his eyes
with hot grease. A taxicab backs up
a one-way street, saving gas. The plastered
walls, the cobblestones still warm us. Boys
kick a soccer ball. A woman carries
a car battery on her head. We see
all this as though we were remembering it,
as though the day had stretched on into March
and we were looking back through months

of transparent air. Above the tower
of San Isidro, a weightless scrap of moon
drifts on the sunset like a shallow boat.

Lullaby after the Rain

It rained all day today.
Now, under the moon's
half-open eye, the mole
noses his way

through the damp loam
under the roots
where the fat grubs sleep.
He's home,

earth muscling
around him wet and warm.
Grubs, say his blind eyes,
grubs and *spring.*

A snail slides through the grass,
antennae pulling in
the news—the massacres
and meannesses

that people sleep with—
takes it in, digests it,
lays it in a thin
silver path

across the walk. Small
repairs, a cottage industry.
Moon eases west and down.
Some petals fall.

Macabre

In the old woodcuts, the leering
skeletons approach and tap us
on the shoulder, cutting in,

requesting the next dance.
The civility of it, the formality—
we dance a few turns to the fluty

music, fingers hooked in rib bones,
then slip off two by two
into the bushes. Getting born

is violent—flesh tearing
and crying out. But dying is
honor your partner

and do-si-do. How nimble
all the moves.
How trim the shrubbery.

Qui Tollis Peccata Mundi

Ordinarily, the rocks pitch down
when they break loose from the chimneys
up on the cliff—pitch down,
smash whatever they come to,
and hiss on into the sea. But this huge
boulder, *peccatum mundi*, rolled slowly,
bouncing on the talus then lumbering into
the forest. We heard it coming. It flattened
pines, lurched through the riverbed
then down here into the heat, shouldered
palms and banana trees like some elephant
with a long memory. It settled on our house,
pushed in the roof. We couldn't stand up.
Had to crawl in, sleep with that boulder
on our chests. We knew it was somebody's
fault. The children grew up under it,
thought houses must be like that. Then
somehow You did it. Lifted it. Took
it away. *Christe. Domine.* We stood again,
breathed, looked out at the sea-swells
carrying blessings our way, bowing
toward us, offering at our feet the rich
foam. *Tollis* is the word, all right.
Restless under the rock, we heard
the air wince as though a bell swung
high overhead, paused with its mouth
wide open, upward, then fell and struck.
It tolled and tolled, its pitch almost
too high for us to hear, or too low,
but we could feel it wrench our flesh—
and, in the rock, crevices opened. Bong.
Bong. And the rock split, crumbled,
fell away. A monkey lifted
a white bromeliad from a branch

and sucked the sweet fruit at its heart.
A parrot shouted. We raised the children
above our heads and danced.

We have restored the roof of our house
and we fish again in the open sea.
Morning fog congeals and runs like mercy
down our arms. Occasionally, clearing
a few yards for squash or beans, we curse
the hacked tangle of roots, the black flies,
curse the heat and our lives, curse
the rutting peccaries that raid our plot.
Only occasionally they come, the peccaries
with their black hair and white lips—
the smoky pork taste of their flesh.

Patricia Hooper

Patricia Hooper was born in Saginaw, Michigan, and received her BA and MA degrees from the University of Michigan. She is the author of two books of poetry, *Other Lives,* which was awarded the Norma Farber First Book Award of the Poetry Society of America, and *At the Corner of the Eye,* which was published in 1997 by Michigan State University Press. She is also the author of a State Street Press chapbook, *The Flowering Trees,* and two children's books. Her poems have appeared in *Poetry,* the *Atlantic Monthly,* the *American Scholar,* the *Hudson Review,* the *Kenyon Review, Ploughshares,* and other magazines. She lives in Bloomfield Township, Michigan.

In the Backyard

This morning a hawk plunges
straight for the squirrel at my feeder
and leaves only
its signature: blood on the snow.

All morning it circled the yard,
then dove, stunning itself
on the glass sky of my window,

and in minutes returned, braving
the thin, perilous channel
between hedgerow and house. I was watching
its path as it fell, its persistence,

and the squirrel, how it dashed
for the downspout, finding itself
motionless under the heat
of the hawk's body,

the claws in its rib cage, the sudden
tearing of wind as it rose
over the fence, the feeder,

the tops of maples and houses.
All morning it stays with me, not
the squirrel's terror, the hawk's
accuracy, but only

how it must feel to be lifted
out of your life, astonished

at the yard growing smaller, the earth
with its snow-covered fields tilting,
and what must be your shadow
flying across it, farther
and farther below.

The Gardener

Since the phlox are dying,
and the daisies with their bright bodies
have shattered in the wind,

I go out among these last dancers,
cutting to the ground the withered asters,
the spent stalks of the lilies, the black rose;

and see them as they were in spring, the time
of eagerness and blossoms, knowing how
they will all sleep and return;

and sweep the dry leaves over them and see
the cold earth take them back as now
I know it is taking me

who have walked so long among them, so amazed,
so dazzled by their brightness I forgot
their distance, how of all

the chosen, all the fallen in the garden,
I was different: I alone
could not come again to the world.

Diligence

A nuthatch is hammering seeds
into the fence post. I heard it
when I opened the front door.

All day yesterday it kept flying
from the feeder to the trees and house.
At first I thought it was a neighbor
tapping in a nail....

Now it's out there in the first cold
morning of the fall.
When I woke, before daylight,
the most disproportionate sadness
came over me,

the one that owned my life
for months last time until some bright
distraction flashed through the air.

Thank heaven another day of earnest
busyness is beginning in the leaves.

Sometimes I wake up
to a grief I can't remember
the cause of, which slips in
under my sleep, and which for days my mind
must have been working desperately to ward off.

Monet's Garden

"I perhaps owe having become a painter to flowers."

Claude Monet

Rainy afternoons
the blues blurred
into each other.
He strolled through
brush strokes: irises
against sky, ponds
filling, a bright
canvas still wet.
Now that he had
flowers to paint
on rainy days
at Giverny, no day
would be wasted.
When sun filled
foxgloves, the bold
cups of red poppies,
he rearranged the effect.
Lifting anemones, moving
nasturtiums nearer
the path, he saw how
everything spilled
over: wild
geraniums poured
into lilies, puddles
of pink saxifrage, waves
of gold grasses. Dissatisfied,
he scraped off the spent
blossoms, added
masses of starry dahlias,
smudges of briar roses
in slow wind. Daily
he "dug, planted,
weeded...evenings
the children watered."
The picture was never
finished: always a new

vista emerged—leaves
shifting, purple
fading to silver, the rose
ripening. Alone in the house,
pleased with the raked
paths, he watched rain
making its alterations.
His hand followed
quickly: columbine
dried in the left
foreground, asters
lifted their bowed heads.
As light became color, sky
vanished behind
foliage, no surface
remained bare. Even
as Camille died, he began
"focusing on her temples—
graded colors which death
was imposing—they were
blue, yellow, grey tones..."
like storm coming over
the garden, like
evening without crimson,
without sienna. At last
there was no horizon, only
a dense canvas painted
to great depth. It was
everywhere: blur
of children or leaves, paths
flowing away through
lindens, his own hand
vanishing as he reached
for a blossom and touched
azure: skies, oceans,
that sea spreading
over him as he sank
into it, into the deep,
inescapable garden.

Photo by Patricia Clay

Murray Jackson

Murray Jackson was born in Philadelphia and grew up on Brush and Canfield in Detroit. He attended Wayne State University, joined the faculty in 1955, and from 1967 to 1970 served as the founding president of Wayne County Community College. In 1971 he joined the faculty of the University of Michigan Center for the Study of Higher Education, from which he retired in 1991 as professor emeritus. In 1980 he was elected to the Wayne State University Board of Governors. His most recent work includes *Watermelon Rinds and Cherry Pits* (Broadside Press) and *Woodland Sketches: Scenes from Childhood* (X-Press Productions). These poems, appearing here for the first time, are part of work in progress, *Bob Weaving Detroit: Running to Catch the Past.*

San Diego Good-Bye

What does an 18-year-old know from Detroit?
First Fight—Jacksaw Arena,
Oxhead McIntosh, White Plains, New York.

He could hit hard.
I was quicker. He punched heavy.
He was always talkin', "eh nigger boy,
where did you get those funny green eyes?
You know you ain't supposed to win."
I couldn't keep my mind on the fight.
"Black boy, I'm beatin' your ass."

He dropped his right to hammer me with his left,
I slipped the punch, landed a left hook to the jaw.
His jaw dropped, splintered,
hung like a door with a missing hinge.
He clutched and fell, whirled upright,
fell again, pawing at his jaw to push the hurt away.
I stood in a corner, ready
to break his face again.

Then I saw his eyes
panicked, hurt, lost.
Blood trickled from his lips
and splattered to the canvas.

I climbed through the ropes for the last time.

Johnny B.

Johnny seemed to be two deep breaths from the joint.
Some friends had been in and out
ready to go again.
Johnny punched out
cut-glass streets they punched him too

Louie da hood, Quiet Sam,
Chicki Sherman, West Side Jim.
Tuxedo Street in Highland Park.
His mother always invited us to tea,
red beans and gravy.

More friends worked the Cavalier Club,
Baccarat, Barboot, some 21.
Anything else small action.
Corky, Bucko, Mac Parshea
were the entry and exit men at the Cavalier.

Sometimes they rode bare knuckle
for the Shark School.
Skilled in the art of persuasion.
Two plus two was not four,
two plus two was four and ten percent.

One afternoon Johnny wanted to go to college.
Came to visit me with Jake his main man.
Good students eager to know.
Assigned as their advisor,
guess I was responsible for some of their learning.

One day during class break,
fifth race Hazel Park.
Serious study, daily racing form, tip sheet.

Johnny interrupted this tense research
to ask me a question about Egyptian art.

We all needed to get out.
Stunned momentarily, I responded
first things first.
The winner of the fifth race,
then, maybe Egyptian art.

Teach Africa

DEDICATED TO ASA HILLIARD

The dark light of Africa
kissed Cleopatra
long before Caesar and Antony
came to her in their white
togas draped with purple lines.

Africa, like the hard wind,
rages, caresses with one stroke of might.
Tell, tell. What was there?
Did one great hand scoop us together?

We know no single tradition.
Not clan to clan, kin to kin,
village to village.

Don't you hear the heft of
ten thousand songs,
splitting the wind to be free?

I, too, hear Africa in America
the song syncopated, transposed.

Things Ain't What They Used to Be

Telling lies older than us, Billy Lamplighter
Stands on the steps of the middle court.
Watches cars and people, thinks of days
When he danced on a forehead or two.
He could dance Billy thought and smiled.

Geechee George, slick black hair, pimp shoes,
A bottle of Jump Steady clutched in his hand
Swings and kicks at a brown spotted dog
Old Pots, the neighborhood pet.

Billy saw Geechee, called him,
"Why you messin' with the dog?"
Geechee grinned, "Cause I wanna, why?
How much you weigh, man?"
Billy stepped back, click-popped his blade
"500 lbs., in your collar, motha."
Geechee's face got heart-attack serious.

"I don wanna see you on the block.
If I do, I'll be on your ass like white on rice."
Popping beads of sweat faster than a foundry worker,
Half looking at Billy, "Yah, Billy, OK look
All I did was kick the dog."
Billy looked at his blade.
"You got one last time to do that."

Detroit Addendum

FOR PHILIP LEVINE

Not Virgil, not Beatrice.
You, Philip, took us on slick city streets oiled to the pimped belch of
    Detroit:
Dodge Main Wyandotte Chemical Ford Rouge Chevrolet Gear & Axle,
in one unbroken line.

Riverrun past burning moat, round sanguine cauldrons,
ending and beginning over again in coke-oven shakeout.
From fiery epicenter black faces, white faces glow red.
We *stare* through words *into fire until* our *eyes are also fire.*
Things passed from hand to hand in darkness,
we, like machines, cannot see.

King Henry's table, seating in split shifts,
neck bones 'n' ribs, corned beef on rye with mustard, kielbasa and raw
    onions.
Philip, I do remember a black man, the Old Boy,
who danced all night at Ford Highland Park,
My Father.

What Work Is is work.

Photo by Amy Howko

Jonathan Johnson

Jonathan Johnson lives in Michigan's Upper Peninsula. He holds bachelor's and master's degrees from Northern Michigan University, and in 1997 received his PhD in English and creative writing from Western Michigan University. His poems have appeared in *Best American Poetry, 1996, Alaska Quarterly, Indiana Review, Mid-American Review, Cimarron Review,* and *Prairie Schooner,* among other publications. His first book of poems, *Mastodon, 80% Complete,* is published by Carnegie Mellon University Press. He has published fiction and essays in *Quarterly West,* the *River Journal,* and *Willow Springs.*

Retirement

Batman is dark and was once from Manhattan.
He calls his seven sections of graze land
The Batman Ranch. Out past the fenceline,
Batman's Caddy blows smoke, slashes of rain
down the mirror when he turns onto 2,
headed for the River Bed, the Horse Thieves'
one-night-only return, and it occurs to
him that this night is exactly what he's
had in mind ever since the day he sold
off his shares—dusk, calves bawling, pint of Old
Crow in the glove box, NO FEAR in pink neon
on his tinted back window, needle down
around ninety. "Heaven," he says out loud,
"I'm an outlaw in heaven. A desert hound."

But his daughter won't see him. She'll cash
his checks but won't return his calls. He calls
her dorm sometimes, late at night from the porch,
smell of dung and sage, the beep . . . his voice stalls,
"when *was* the last time I saw your blue eyes?
Won't you fly out Sweetheart? Give a little hope?"
And, as he starts the climb up Hal's Pass,
into clouds, the last spring snow on the slopes,
Batman wonders, for the first time in his life,
if he has earned his daughter's contempt, if,
maybe, everyone ought to despise him,
not so much for leaving, but for those times
when he hated all of them, the city
above his cave, full of small fires and pity.

510

The smell of diesel, then tail lights flickering
through trees. I'm not especially handsome or optimistic.
I'm just the man in the pickup behind the bus,
not even a regular on this road, so when the girl
in the last seat flips her notebook open, scrawls
a message, and holds it up to the back window,
I expect only *FUCK OFF*. Pulling closer I read *HI*.
Her slight, closed lips smile through the dirty
back window. Someone has cut her hair straight
at her shoulders. Freckles splash across her nose
and forehead. And I'm suddenly sorry I said
I'm not optimistic, sorry to have begun ungratefully.
After all, this is the road for starting over.
This is the world of cheap acres and possibility,
where high-school kids ride the North Bus
winding its low gears up the Yellow Dog Valley,
dust rising from the washboard, dust falling
like talcum on the spruce and birch in their wake,
dust falling sun-baked on my hood. So just what am I
doing here? What will I know when I know this?
The road is called the 510. No carved-oak cottage signs
up here, no neat, red, newspaper boxes hanging
from thin brass chains above buckets of snapdragons—
just mail boxes every few miles, leaning precariously
over the road. Every week or two I'm back,
dropping it into four-wheel where the pavement ends,
USGS map rolled on the dash, six-pack of RC
on the seat beside me. Once, dawn came down
like a lynx sniffing her way off the ridge,
sniffing cautiously, muscles tense, around the truck.
Lost on a logging spur, I'd parked in the middle
of a thousand-acre clearcut and fell asleep, blue-
green aurora burning above my windshield. This place,
hundreds of empty, scrub square miles, asks nothing.
The Pup Creek asks nothing and spills over granite,
if I abandon my life or not. The old, inevitable Pup.

Something about its storyline—lower elevations and
open, colder water, bronze water pushing into lake-blue.
The freckled kid presses her beautiful, forgiving
syllable to the glass. But why say *forgiving*?
She has concerns of her own, and you must suspect by now
that the aurora burns brighter somewhere else,
somewhere where the roads have woodsy names
and this poem might be read—say down around Shelter Bay
where bright new Jeeps tuck themselves into garages,
and the moose are more frequent, crossing lawns
below honey-brown log homes, heading down
to the Bog Preserve and virgin white pine.
But you must believe me when I tell you
that—charmed beyond the usual solitude—
I roll down the window and wave. *HI* her sign says.
HI as we ride, smiling, watching each other
through the glass and dusty air, into no other mountains
but these. *HI HI HI* shuddering and bouncing
with the yellow bus over washboard. There is a word
for what we have, and the word is optimism.

Shipping Papers

Ten miles off Keweenaw Point the world's a storm,
the port behind us a cancerous hole in my sleep.

Drunk and trying not to let it show, sure as the stoplights
that change over empty road, frat kids head back

up to school from a snowy night at the Duluth dock bars,
and the longshoremen who cast us off this morning

are limping their sagging pickups home, licenses long suspended,
every cop cruiser lurking down the street with the future.

Little difference the details make now, ice on cable rails
thick and smooth as a woman's wrists. Waves spend themselves on our
    hull,

spray fifty feet up into the night through a searchlight beam
scanning the whitecaps ahead, as if it could spot

ourselves among the swells, though we're a clean mile
over a channel cut into the quartzite floor of Superior

by blind, southbound glaciers that have retreated
and wait us out. Something about this work

eliminates the ability to imagine pain beyond your own.
I wait for the wave that crashes through.

Company policy keeps us off the deck during high seas,
locked in a darkened mess where a wall of windows

scrolls the storm over the ship like film. Days and nights
hang around my neck. The past beyond our wake folds closed

and swells and night tries to cover our waking world.
The Duluth Power Station Pond is home to hold-over Canada geese
    who warm their feet

through winter and trot up to people who bring them bread.
I stuffed one in a sack, plump and squirming as dawn rose off the lake.

The cook did him in, and we ate him. I haven't eaten
that well since Toledo. Once, I had better explanations.

Changes in the water answer the sky. We draw deep,
belly oared down with a billion pellets of iron.

In a gale there is no horizon to hope toward,
only the greedy, relentless wind of exactly this spot.

The Indiana Harbor rolls swells over her back like no boat I've
worked, her hundred foot coal boom down along her spine,

red lights and girders like the windblasted radio towers
I watched from my childhood bedroom window, knowing

they relayed words from the past. Any motion, even radio
waves, takes time, and truth comes after the fact.

Arnold Johnston

Arnold Johnston lives in Kalamazoo, Michigan, where he is chairman of the English department and teaches in the creative writing program at Western Michigan University. A collection of his poetry, *What the Earth Taught Us*, was recently published by March Street Press. His other works include *The Witching Voice: A Play about Robert Burns* (Western Michigan University Press, 1973) and *Of Earth and Darkness: The Novels of William Golding* (University of Missouri Press, 1980). On his 1997 CD, *Jacques Brel: I'm Here!* (Western Michigan University), he performs his own translations of songs by the noted Belgian singer-songwriter. Arnie's plays, and others written in collaboration with his wife, Deborah Ann Percy, have won awards, production, and publication across the country. These include *Rasputin in New York*, recently published in an English/Romanian edition by Editura HP (Bucharest), with Romanian translations by Dona Roșu and Luciana Costea. A member of the Dramatists Guild, he is also a resident playwright with the off-off Broadway company AAI Productions.

Spectators As We Are

Sleet patters across my car's window
In the South Beach parking lot. Sitting
Here, hand in hand, we lament spring's slow
Sweep up the coastline from Chicago.

You're not sure I want to be with you;
You know I'm capable of running,
And you're angry. You point out how few
Years we may have, and I can't argue.

You press on: "We should think of each day
As the last gift we'll get." I'm nodding,
But I know we seldom find a way
To live our lives like that. And I say,

"We're never ready for disaster."
For even when we know what's coming,
Foreknowledge never helps us master
Our fate. Like the poor drunk bastard

At the local winefest; the bozo
Thought he'd end the night's fun by walking
Around the city parking ramp's low
Parapet. Falling, he said, "Oh, no."

Could it be he really didn't know,
Despite his friends' and his wife's pleading,
That he might plunge sixty feet onto
The dark pavement down there? And if so,

Can his brief fall convince us that we,
Ourselves, when life finds us performing
Our own crazy stunts, will probably
Feel the same thrill of surprise to be

Dying, too? How can it slip our minds,
Or can a part of us be lying,
That we forget how frail a tie binds
Us to the real world? What is it blinds

Us at such moments? Perhaps the sense
That we're immortal, or just watching
Our own lives, as if experience
Might be a TV show, more intense,

Perhaps, but no more real. Remember
The man who was videotaping
Skydivers, and who, as their 'chutes were
Blossoming below in the cold air,

Stepped out to join them? What the tape shows
Is the cameraman's realizing
That he has no 'chute. We know he knows
When he looks down and the picture goes

Crazy. As long as nothing is real
The camera's focused, recording
Everything; but when he starts to feel
For his ripcord and his veins congeal,

He spurns vision like a false lover.
And now we sit together, watching
Lake Michigan from the dry cover
Of my Toyota. Seagulls hover

Above the waves that attack the dock,
Neither birds nor gray water caring
About us or each other. We talk
Of all this, and of people who walk

Out on the pier to see the lake's show
Of power, despite weather warnings
And common sense. Now and then, we know,
Someone's swept away and sucked below,

Battered by the waves, and drowned. And I
Wonder if, when they find they're breathing
Water and know they're about to die,
They spend a moment wondering why

Their lives seemed like something they had paid
To watch, all the moments unfolding
Like someone else's story. "They made
The choices," you say. "They could have stayed

Where they were safe and warm. Whatever
They believed, life wasn't happening
To them. We make it happen. Never
Forget that. You can be too clever

On the subject, brood too much over
Whys and wherefores, and avoid choosing
Your own turning points: wife or lover,
Here or there. You know you can't cover

All the bets. You can't have certainty;
It's all a risk. There's no real knowing
Till you try. Some risks are bad, but we
Aren't one of them. So there." That's me

All over, as you know, spectator
And recorder, but seldom acting
For myself, habitual waiter
On eventual turns of fate or

Chance. So I'm the one I'm speaking of,
Who thinks life can be lived by waiting
For someone else to decide when love
Is over. My doubt goes hand in glove

With your certainty. And yet we lay
This morning on the beach, sheltering
Behind a low dune, watching the way
Snow formed brief stars on your coat. You'd say

It's the best image I could have drawn.
With that thought, I start the car. Nearing
The road, we glance back at the lake. One
Gull hangs there. You smile. And I drive on.

Syzygy in Center Field

syzygy: 1. in astronomy, either of two opposing points in
the orbit of a heavenly body. 2. in ancient prosody, a group
of two feet, as a dipody.

"We will be called The Syzygies"

Norman Kurilik, softball manager

We can't lose this one.
I believe that, standing here in center field,
Watching Tony suck up grounders,
Gun the ball to Norm at first,
Bill pounding down the line from third
Under a soft foul fly,
Rob pivoting from second for the quick d.p.
Every now and then Jeff fungoes one
And I move, easy, under the high arc,
Another can of corn.
Or Stu pinwheels after a liner,
Snags it, waves his glove,
An ice-cream cone.
The fat guy's catcalls from the bleachers—
What does he know?

But the games came and went.
Sudden grounders skimmed across the field,
Caromed off legs and forearms;
Our pegs bounced in to second or to third.
Long flies and bloopers dropped among us,
Heavy as stones. Home plate acquired,
From passing feet, a layer of dust
No ump could ever brush away.
I watched it all from center field
Then right, that grave for guys the manager
Wants buried, and finally behind the plate,
Squatting like a backstop Buddha,
Meditating on those last indignities:
The coach's box; the bench.

Most of us are gone now:
Tony to a different hot-dog stand,
Bill to Wichita and dreams of Nashville,
Stu to slide those bad knees under a typewriter.
Only Jeff's still out there, cracking the long ones,
And Norm, still searching in his bones
For Sparky Anderson and Pee Wee Reese.
Now I run in place, do sit-ups, dumbbell curls,
Still in shape, but off the basepaths.
Like the fat guy in the bleachers
I begin to forget what a bat feels like,
And to learn what he knew all along:
We can't win this one.

Laura Kasischke

Laura Kasischke is the author of three collections of poems: *Wild Brides* (New York University Press, 1992), *Housekeeping in a Dream* (Carnegie Mellon University Press, 1995), and *Fire & Flower* (Alice James Books, 1998), and two novels: *Suspicious River* (Houghton Mifflin, 1996) and *White Bird in a Blizzard* (Hyperion, 1999). She has received grants from the National Endowment for the Arts, the Alice Fay DiCastagnola Award from the Poetry Society of America, and two Pushcart Prizes. She teaches creative writing at Washtenaw Community College and lives in Chelsea, Michigan.

Cocktail Waitress

Things change, but those days
my tray was always full

of damp blue veils, amazing

scarves of waste things washed
up gasping between the waves
as I ran into the future with them, the way

a child might run toward her mother
with wet hair like weeds
sopping in her hands
one morning at the beach. I still believed

the day would come
when I would bump straight into love
in a barroom, like
a businessman with wings. Later

I'd loosen his red noose
in a mildewed room
of the Holiday Inn, un-
button his stiff shirt

and there those wings would be, soft
and alive, two

wet white hens, cool
or clammy
under my hands. Half

skin, half
tissue paper smelling
like fresh and restless paste. They'd

tense and tremble
when I touched them, stunted

gulls with nowhere
to go, while my
fish-net stockings, strung
up, dripped
above the tub. But my

father called my roommates
the False Hope Club. Five
ephemeral station wagons idling, five
lilac blossoms browning

on the sidewalk, five
unsolved murders just
waiting to occur. We

lounged around in lipstick while the sky
rippled its
blue metallic dime-store slip outside, while

the heiress starved to death below us, and the thin
blondes above us made a feast
of water every night
by their TV. Once
we found a life-sized plastic doll

strung up behind our dumpster, like
a sacrifice to nothing, a dagger

through her heart, and down the block

a muddy set of women's
underwear was found
beneath some cardboard in a barn. My
father thought it was a warning
from our landlord, but I
still believed in miracles
and spirits of every kind, believed
one day I'd find a man who'd pant
and struggle

in a victory garden—mine—
snagged in vegetation, coiled

vines around his wrists. His
lush hair would be bleached
green, and there might even be

pumpkins swollen like awful
god-heads at his feet, or
overgrown suns—while my

figment fell and rose around him, a foil
screen, while my

melancholy figment
sipped a margarita

and filed her fingernails to speartips

in the future by his pool.

My Heart

When August was finally done, his
wife never mailed the dark
card to me that said, "Hon

he's all yours now, good
luck and happy Labor Day," and still
I *loved* that man, the way

magnolias go
sloppy and wet as pneumonia
on front lawns when summer's over, the way
a cool moon might appear on a bright September afternoon
to the naked eye to be
just a blind blue infant face

hovering in space. Those
human trees: Listen
to them wheeze all night in sleep while

the washing machine churns blood
and whiskey out of your sheets. I
loved that man, whatever that means.

Whatever you need, I thought.
Whatever you eat. GOTCHA
he wrote one morning

in red pen above my breast. Bull's-eye
where my heart was, and the earth
bobbed a bit

on the little string that holds it
over a whoosh of air
and emptiness, the way

when I was a child a magician pulled
a long silk scarf
from my ear. I could hear

red wind when it passed
out of me into his hands. All
the other children at this party

gasped, but I
knew where he'd gotten it from, and felt
my heart spin in me like a sparking

toy when he was done.

Photo by Lisa Powers

Josie Kearns

Josie Kearns was born in Flint, Michigan, and has won three Hopwood Awards and four Creative Artist Awards from the Michigan Council for the Arts (ArtServe). Her work appears in magazines such as *Georgia Review, Iowa Review,* and *Poetry Northwest* and was recently anthologized in *Boomer Girls* from University of Iowa Press.

She has won several fellowships, as well as artist residencies at Ragdale Foundation in Lake Forest, Illinois. She served as a fellow for the National Endowment for the Arts in 1989.

Life after the Line (nonfiction) was published by Wayne State University Press and her new book of poems, *New Numbers,* was published in March 2000 by New Issues Press. She teaches writing and literature at the University of Michigan in Ann Arbor.

New Numbers

"For the Maya, each number had identity and was
itself a god."

—*Empires of Time*, p.189

FOR DAVID ORLOWSKI

Xelah Xalong

The number of instant karma
and the Chinese fire horse
the number of the names of gods
and what Pandora found
in the box engraved on the emerald:
That which is too beautiful to be named.

If this is your number
you have been saved from drowning
you have saved someone from fire
you were somehow not on the plane
that crashed in Europe.
You carry this number inside yourself:
It is not next.

You know who-done-it, that she
is in Paraguay, how her partner
will be caught.
If this is your number
you smell like absinthe.
If this is your number
the stranger at the bus stop asks you
if it is okay to embezzle
his wife's fortune and leave her
and her lover for Aruba and forgiveness.
If this is your number you know whether or not
To tell him she will follow.

You catch the quicksilver glimmer
of the last Perseod meteor shower.
Stars wink open over your ceiling every night
if this is your number:
You bear true witness,
The palms of your hands are diaries.

Quaro
is the number beyond knowing.
Out there in the Milky Way on the event horizon
of an infinite continuum.

Quaro is the thoughts in the universe.
Quaro redefines pi.
Quaro is not for everyone.

As unknowable as souls.
As uncontrived as gravity.
Quaro is the number of times you will be
remembered after you die
and the number of your rebirths.
It is said:
Not even the moon knows Quaro.

"Quaro," a mother says.
But not yours, this mother in the future
where Quaro is discussed as commonly
as how rain forests regenerate
through a thousand years of peace.

That mother says to her child
"If you knew quaro
the piñata of sky
would open up
and break down all the stars for you."

Hystra

Choosing the day I'd live over is simple:
my mother's 39th birthday
when I rode my Schwinn like a schooner
down cracks of breakneck driveways,

>   *This is the placeholder:*
>   *The cache of souls unopened,*
>   *Bernadette's letter sealed.*

Six streets over to the Ben Franklin's
to buy with my own dollar the thin, glass-blown
chalices, one-use-only, "Fragrances of the World":

>   *An isotope zero*
>   *where your fused and unfused life*
>   *becomes matrix.*

Evening in Paris, Tigress, Ambush, Tabu
titles as dangerous as the 7-Up and chablis mix
she sometimes let me sip at parties
as she would this night.

>   *A continuum of ladder and hinge:*
>   *what swings there*
>   *not even the moon*
>   *knows the end of*

where mounds of potato salad and rhubarb pie
and the blueberry cake Aunt Ann baked that day
would greet her with my step-father, Ray's, gift
of the double-sink kitchen cabinets when we shouted

>   *as a plutonium zero*
>   *as a cascade*
>   *woven by the dead*

"Surprise!" and her loam brown eyes
misted over and I was still
nine or ten

    like a pressure valve
    an airlock wheel
    on a submarine

And the cards of canasta and gin rummy
the Old Grandad whiskey bottle, never empty
(by which I mean Ray did not drink
like my father)

    The last Chinese box
    in the long tradition of boxes.
    The door that is a box.

my brother-in-law and step-father sitting
at the yellow and chrome kitchen table
and the lumber soon to be painted
"redwood" stacked outside like bonds
to ensure a future of perfect fences

    1066
    November 22, 1963
    Cinque de Mayo
    2001

where it fell to these men, white
t-shirted and overalled, to pound in the poles
of that fence as if this life would stay
where we put it.

    the Secret Annex
    never found

And I fell
asleep that night under

that same table listening to the grinding
of stories my aunts told, voices weaving
a thick canopy, lifting me toward sleep

> *our private compartment*
> *your false wall, hidden spring*
> *survival kit*

in a language as foreign and majestic
as Lima, Peru, I learned about that morning
second hour geography class

> *rough diamonds*
> *in the 1930's coat sleeve*
> *lined in black taffeta*

that night I dreamed
my bed was the shape of Peru
landlocked, yet water kept
seeping in, monsoon

> *the bubble of time*
> *between moments*
> *the planck numeral*

In the middle of that night
under the table they almost
didn't find me

> *This is Hystra the trapdoor*
> *Hystra the dice*
> *in your unbroken life.*

as if I'd disappeared
through a doorway
into now.

Gerry LaFemina

The author of five collections of poetry including *A Print of Wildflowers* and *Shattered Hours: Poems 1988–94*, Gerry LaFemina lives in Grayling, Michigan, and teaches at Kirtland Community College, where he founded the first AFA Creative Writing Program in the country. The recipient of an ArtServe Michigan Creative Artist Grant and an Irving Gilmore Emerging Artist Fellowship, he edits the national literary magazine *Controlled Burn*.

The Raccoon

At first we saw her tracks: the scattered scads
of scat around the yard's perimeter and trails
of little paw prints, seemingly fossilized

in drying mud. Then we heard her, trapped in the metal trash
can, rattling the scraps of a supper long forgotten
and snacks of chips with salsa; chocolate

chip cookies; midnight omelettes. Eventually, we saw her
hours past dawn, raised on hind legs, head in the garbage
again. Some said she must be dangerous—maybe rabid—

to be out in daylight, and they wanted to call
the parks department or the sheriff, but we believed
different, understood what a cruel god hunger

can be, demanding we find food no matter what the risk.
And yes, I've dined
and dashed. Twice. The first time I was 18 and cool,

exiting through the glass door of the diner
and glimpsed only for a brief interlude the counterman's
countenance—part dismay, part rage. And the lady

I collided on the sidewalk? Her shocked *Oh*
fused with the whoosh of the door closing
and together they cloaked whatever

he may have said as I vanished
among the other leather coats across the avenue
in needle park. A decade later

I returned and tried to decipher the paisley patterns
of grease painted on the waiter's apron,
tried to read in the erosion of his face

if he had been there that Saturday evening.
And what could I do but pay
double then, seeming without reason. The second time I ran

from a restaurant's register, I was older and poor.
I left a cigarette building its ceremonial mound
in a golden glass ashtray. I admit: I felt no shame

nor guilt, just a slight second of empathy
for the waitress, who may have cursed me the remainder of her day,
even when starting her seven year old station wagon

that evening, stomping the accelerator twice
before turning the key. She didn't see me
on the bench across the street—my camouflage

of tobacco smoke. Or she chose
to ignore me, much like that raccoon we saw daily,
night or day, which ignored the tires of too close Kilgore Avenue

and suffered the misdemeanors of the flesh.
And yes—I fed her; everyday
I hefted a bowl of sweet cereal, left it beside the door

and watched through a window
as she ate the red, green, and yellow rings.
I carried that bowl out

despite complaining neighbors—despite, even,
the continuation of raids against my trash.
I carried that bowl in my supplicant's fingers

like a present or an offering
for benevolence. I carried it forward
as if it were sacred.

Poem with Wisteria Growing along Its Margin

The five cool stars above this town look down
upon the main drag and the bar where a guy once fired
four bullets into a biker who had said nothing

to the man, who had just laughed too loud and at an inappropriate
    moment.
The first shot sounded like the break
of an eight-ball rack, but louder
                    more resonant. The subsequent squeezes
of the trigger—redundant, more resounding

as they mixed with the shrieks of beer-drinkers.
Hysteria spreading among them like wisteria

along a garden fence; its occasional balloons of violet
flowering vividly in the green mesh of its leaves. And I remember

lying in such a garden.
Remember the lush cologne of pollen and the garnet bees
buzzing their cargo routes between blossoms
and a distant apiary.

       ∽

                 And I thought there was nobody else
in that garden, so I was surprised then, when walking its paths later,
to hear weeping. I was amazed
by how sudden and communicable sadness can be—

and how embarrassed the woman became when she glanced up
to see me standing there, the white heart
of a wisteria blossom barely beating in my extended hand. She shook
her head and smiled.

Her face so fragile I thought she'd shatter
or break into flower.

~

Consider the ordinance of griefs:
should one begin with the phenomenal or the ordinary?

I count them on the threads of my shirt
and on the gem-like sparkling of dust

in the slide of light that entrusts itself to my vision.
Then I lose track, distracted by a concert of ambulances and police
    cruisers:
their cacophonic call-and-response.

~

The next morning I heard how the biker's wife insisted
—insisted that was the paper's word—it was all her fault:

she had wanted to go out that night.
And her husband, because he loved her
and because it was a lovely October evening and he knew soon he'd
    have

to stow the Harleys away for the winter, because of these things
he agreed although it was a weeknight
and there'd be an early morning driving a propane truck the next day.
The jukebox was shaking AC/DC's "Shook Me All Night Long"

and he had just gotten up for another round . . . .
She never mentions the expression on his face, mouth agape,
suddenly soundless. Then the remaining patrons screaming.

~

And after the questioning
and after the gunman took his position in the back seat
of a squad car and shrank
to two dimensions with its slamming door, the officers let the bartender
    back inside
and the owners. The three men sat at a table and one of them
poured whiskey into tall tumblers cored with ice. Nobody spoke.

And when they finished their drinks
they simultaneously stood, and, still speechless,
went about cleaning up: one of them counting the till;

the others filling buckets with rags and suds
to start removing blood from the walls and carpet—
a task they knew to be futile

but necessary
like this poem in the end, whatever
its message.

$\sim$

                                      I remember how weeks passed and still his bike,
a 67 roadster, stood outside the bar
reverent as a statue.

Then it was gone although nobody knew where it went
or who took it. But I last saw it

parked there beneath a thin skin of fresh powder
and the splayed glove of light from the bar's bay window.
Inside: a small splatter of what may have been blood
blemished the pool table felt like a location on a map

you can't return to, and the new barman
polished the heavy glass mugs with a rag while outside
the snow wafted scattershot like blossoms
on a dark wall of ivy.

David Dodd Lee

David Dodd Lee grew up in Muskegon, Michigan. His publications include poems in *Sycamore Review, Cutbank, Puerto del Sol,* the *Quarterly, Green Mountains Review,* and *Permafrost.* A selection of his work was included in *The PrePress Awards, 1992–93.* A chapbook, *Counting Backwards,* was published in 1999, and another, entitled *Wilderness,* is forthcoming from March Street Press. A full-length collection, *Downsides of Fish Culture,* appeared in 1997, published by New Issues Press. He is the former poetry editor of *Third Coast,* and was associate poetry editor at *Passages North* for several years. He presently lives in Kalamazoo, where he works as a freelance editor.

Death on U.S. 131

I remember one summer
standing in deep grass near a big tree
and thinking *I am just so happy...*
Well, okay. But later I became this *dark person.*
Just being alive counts for something,
I'm happy about that.
I ice fish occasionally and that gives me pleasure—
a big pike alive on the snow.
But the snow doesn't move me.
I stand back at car wrecks, secretly amazed.
On the highway once a dead woman
spoke to me. I almost thought
she must be comfortable
broken beyond decision
on the warm asphalt she claimed for herself.
The radiators hissed in the background like stage props.
I touched her right hand.
She died right while I was looking at her.
She was worried about her baby
who it turned out was fine, oblivious,
strapped snugly in his car seat,
but she was gone before anyone could tell
her that. In the meantime
the rest of us go on breathing.
Life and death, snap your fingers.
Sometimes I think, *There's a bluebird
on a branch.* I love the words.
But the bird—when you actually see one—
is the blue of the human eye,
flickering, going down.

Cigarette Break

It's not the weather, or the fact that two ambulances
have already unloaded their cargo and sit in the emergency drive,
idling. It's sunny, in fact, out here, next to this brick
wall where I'm taking time out for a cigarette
and a cup of coffee, freezing my ass off actually, but happy,
for a few seconds at least, to be out of the basement.
It's not very much, one cigarette, and it's not very heartening
watching sick people struggle through the snow
to smoke one either. Wrapped in an oversized coat,
a woman whose spindly legs are bare where they meet
her inadequately slippered feet, limps by trailing an I.V.
that dangles from a portable stand. Whatever I've got waiting
downstairs—the anesthesia cart to inventory, some cardboard boxes
to bale—takes half an hour. I hate that I hate what I do,
but not because of this sick woman, who,
after feeling her pockets, jabs her chin at me to ask for a light.
She's ugly, and old, a hank of greasy hair
and a mouthful of broken-up teeth. And she won't talk,
doesn't want to I guess. She sucks the flame into her cigarette,
takes a long initial drag, then blows out the smoke.
She stands there hunched over, smoking, and clutching the I.V. stand
for support. I've been at this job a long time, so this woman's
nothing, one of the legion soon-to-be-dead.
One woman expired, right here, last fall, fell over in the middle
of a sentence. They rushed her into the ER on one of the brand
new rolling stretchers, but I heard later she had died almost instantly
from a burst aorta. No big surprise when you work at a hospital.
The sick come in. The sick go out. Some of them don't go out.
In the meantime all the healthy people stand around
glimpsing the future, their eyes lit up like a deer's in traffic.
Occasionally a visitor will wail for their dead, a howl
you can hear coming through the vents in the storeroom.
It sounds like someone burning in an empty room.
I know I should quit these goddamned cigarettes. But they buy me
    some time,

somehow, a momentary stay of execution. Then it's
back to the business of filling up bins. I flick my smoke into a snow
    drift.
And the woman, who's suddenly listing a little, begins hacking,
doing her best to split her thick winter coat. When she finally
recovers she turns to look at me, watching her.
Her eyes are red, wet looking.
It happens again and again, the dead look out of their graves
at the living, not a word needing to be uttered.

A Poem about Blue Gills

There are poems about blue gills. There are poems
about trout. The blue gill doesn't give a shit.
It'll eat a bare hook but would rather not hear
about your childhood. The blue gill's thick headed.
It hunkers down in the weeds, thinking. The trout's like a young girl
in a wedding gown. Touch it and it dies.
You can pull a blue gill out a pike's ass, it might
still swim away. I'm not talking about pumpkinseeds,
those little flecks of tinsel. The blue gill's
the stud of all panfish. People catch pumpkinseeds
thinking they're blue gills. A pumpkinseed shivers;
it thinks it's going to convince you it's cold.
Blue gills are fatalists. A slab in your hand may jerk its head
twice. Once hooked it goes for the mud. By the time
it's resting on a flotation device it's willing to die.
It doesn't grope like a rock bass, swallowing air,
the blue gill's a realist. It knows it's just a wedge of painted flesh,
heavy enough to pull you half out of the boat.
If you've got a big white bucket of panfish
sitting on top of the ice, the blue gill's the one still living,
thinking, its head like a stapler, saying its prayers.

Three Stories about Owls

The owls, two of them, handle all the branches in the chinkapin.
They edge through the tree
with their eyes open.
When I come near they fly off
and I dream of a naked girl smoking in bed.
I can hear in the snowy silence the sound of their gizzards grinding
the bones and hearts and light-struck eyes.

～

The corn stalks suck up rain, then stand freezing in the cold air and
    sun.
They become gnarled, like my elderly neighbors,
amidst stacks of rusty bed springs spattered with chicken shit,
their robes and slips tearing in the wind.

In winter their windows ping in the sub-zero nights,
a sound like the chains pulling the bones
of our dead livestock through the fields hung with lanterns.
A girl and a boy undress and kneel in cold milk.
The electric fence purrs. The old man makes love to his wife on a
    blanket of leaves
surrounded by pumpkins and Indian corn,
the T.V. crackling in the corner. When one of the local owls is struck
    by a car,
the woman, feeling a chill, moves over her husband, straddling him,
and opens the bedroom window,
which suddenly goes silent, warming up, ice crystals hissing alive
    through the screen
and onto her sexual body.

～

My lover has a ruler-sized scar
running like a creek
over her shoulder blade, through the valley
where her spine slopes toward her buttocks.
In the morning

it looks like a small mountain range,
red with white peaks.
I like to soothe her with aloe.
Whenever she brings a wounded owl
into our home
the deer out back stop trampling
the snow, their eyes reflecting back
the color of branch water.
I remember hanging naked
from a cyclone fence, my wrists bound with twine.
Somewhere a radio played "Rock & Roll, Part Two,"
which is now a sports anthem.
The two track was lined with candles.
Anyway, the aspens argued beautifully
in the dusky breeze,
and a huge owl, infested with louse-fly larvae,
beat its large wings and growled.
The moon sailed through the sky like a schooner.
In this town we have the magic of tidal pools
and gravitational reversals
and the tamaracks exude what we call "tears,"
liquid the color of skim milk.
My lover exhales the smoke of her cigarette
over the cups of my privacy.
You're a beautiful child, she says.

Photo by Joe Vaughn

Thomas Lynch

Thomas Lynch is the author of three collections of poems, most recently *Still Life in Milford* (W. W. Norton, 1998). A collection of his essays, *The Undertaking—Life Studies from the Dismal Trade* (W. W. Norton, 1997), was a finalist for the National Book Award and won the American Book Award for nonfiction and the Heartland Prize. His work appears in the *New Yorker, Harpers,* the *New York Times, Paris Review, Poetry,* and throughout the U.K. and Ireland. He lives and works in Milford, Michigan, where he is the funeral director.

An Evening Walk to the Sea by Friesians

So much in this place comes in black and white—
the cattle and clergy, magpies, the stars and dark,
those crisp arithmetics for how things are:
one for sorrow, two for joy, three to marry, four, five...
or the tally of Shalts and Thou Shalt Nots.
Despite the stars' vast evidence, we count.

A score of Michael Murray's Friesian calves
lift their faces from their pasturage
to stand and watch me standing, watching back,
my stillness and their stillness counterbalancing.
I'm making for the cliffs to fish for mackerel
to share with neighbors over evening tea.

And on these yearling hides, like seas and continents,
a random mapwork that yet articulates
a world of hard borders, sharp opposites,
clear options where the right is manifest,
the kindly husbandry of what is obvious.
Suspect of certainties, I watch the tides—

their comings and their goings, rise and fall,
the edges of approach and leave-taking
in constant motion, changing constantly
the division of ocean and landfall.
Likewise the evening light, likewise the line
between the seascape and the darkening sky

where mountains or cloudbanks or maybe islands blur
into a frontier without horizons.
God's Will, like anyone's guess at the weather,
the count we keep of certain birds, the firmament,
bright fish, the cows in their now distant fields, astray:
whatever comes in black and white goes grey.

Bishop's Island

Two holy men came out here long ago
and prayed against the ground that bound them to
the green mainland and their prayers were answered.
Thus, from their rock in the North Atlantic
they watched for God among such signs and wonders
as sea and sky and wind and dark supply:
fury and firmament and privations
enough to dull the flesh, and beauty too,
to break the heart. They wept with gratitude,
kept silent, built an oratory. There,
you can see the ruins of it from the coast road.
Sea birds brought them mackerel it is said.
Fresh water sprung from the rock. When one died
the other buried him and cut a stone
then died himself some few years after that.
And everything was swept—his hut, his bones—
into the vast ocean and was forgot
until some bishop on a pilgrimage
centuries later, as bishops often did,
declared them saints, proclaimed the holy island his.

The Old Operating Theatre, London

To rooms like this old resurrectionists
returned the bodies they had disinterred—
fresh corpses so fledgling anatomists
could study Origin & Insertion points
of deltoids, pecs, trapezius and count
the vertebrae, the ball & socket joints.
And learn the private parts and Latin names
by which the heart becomes a myocardium,
the high cheek bone, a zygoma, the brain,
less prone to daydream as a cerebellum.

And squirming in their stiff, unflinching seats,
apprentice surgeons witnessed, in the round,
new methods in advanced colostomy,
the amputation of gangrenous limbs
and watched as Viennese lobotomists
banished the ravings of a raving man
but left him scarred and drooling in a way
that made them wonder was he much improved?
But here the bloodied masters taught dispassionate
incisions—how to suture and remove.

In rooms like this, the Greeks and Romans staged
their early dramas. Early Christians knelt
and hummed their liturgies when it was held
that prayer and penance were the only potions.
Ever since Abraham, guided by God,
first told his tribesmen of the deal he'd made—
their foreskins for that ancient Covenant—
good medicine's meant letting human blood.
Good props include the table and the blade.
Good theatre is knowing where to cut.

Still Life in Milford—
Oil On Canvas by Lester Johnson

You're lucky to live in a town like this
with art museums and Indian food
and movie houses showing foreign films
and grad-students and comely undergrads.
Years back I'd often make the half-hour trip.
It was good for my creative juices
to browse the holy books at Shaman Drum.
Still, life in Milford isn't all that bad.

We have two trendy restaurants and a bar
well known by locals for its Coney dogs.
We have a book shop now. We even have
a rush hour, art fairs and bon vivants.
And a classic car show every October—
mostly muscle cars—Dodges, Chevys, Fords.
No psychic healers yet or homeopaths.
Still, life in Milford has a certain ambiance,

more Wyeth than Picasso, to be sure,
more meatloaf and potatoes than dim-sum. Fact is,
at first I thought this Lester Johnson was
a shirt-tail cousin of the Johnson brothers—
long-standing members of the Chamber of Commerce
in Milford, Michigan, like me. In fact
his only connection to these parts was
Still Life in Milford, gathering dust here

in the basement of the art museum.
His own Milford's somewhere back east, near Yale—
the day job, teaching, he could never quit
the way that Robert Frost taught English here
and Donald Hall before the muse in them
escaped their offices in Angell Hall.
They were last seen running and may be running still.
Life in Milford, Michigan is similar.

I have steady work, a circle of friends
and lunch on Thursdays with the Rotary.
I have a wife, unspeakably beautiful,
a daughter and three sons, a cat, a car,
good credit, taxes, and mortgage payments
and certain duties here. Notably,
when folks get horizontal, breathless, still:
life in Milford ends. They call. I send a car.

Between the obsequies I play with words.
I count the sounds and syllables and rhymes.
I try to give it shape and sense, like so:
eight stanzas of eight lines apiece, let's say
ten syllables per line or twelve. Just words.
And if rhyming's out of fashion, I fashion rhymes
that keep their distance, four lines apart, like so.
Still, life in Milford keeps repeating. Say

I'm just like Lester, just like Frost and Hall:
I covet the moment in which nothing moves
and crave the life free of life's distractions.
A bucket of flowers on a table.
A vase to arrange the flowers in. A small
pipe—is it?—smoldering in an ashtray to
suggest the artist and impending action.
Still Life in Milford seems a parable

on the human hunger for creation.
The flowers move from bucket to vase
like moving words at random into song—
the act of ordering is all the same—
the ordinary becomes a celebration.
Whether paper, canvas, ink or oil paints,
once finished we achieve a peace we call
Still Life in Milford. Then we sign our names.

Naomi Long Madgett

Naomi Long Madgett's career as a published poet spans more than five decades and includes eight volumes. The most recent are *Exits and Entrances* (Lotus Press), the award-winning *Octavia and Other Poems* (Third World Press), and *Remembrances of Spring: Collected Early Poems* (Michigan State University Press). *A Poet's Voice,* a documentary film produced by Vander Films and based on "Octavia," won the Gold Apple Award for Excellence in 1999 from the National Educational Media Network and was nominated for an Emmy. Her poems have appeared in numerous journals and over 160 anthologies in the U.S. and Europe. She has also edited two anthologies, including *Adam of Ifé: Black Women in Praise of Black Men.*

Among her numerous awards are an American Book Award and the Michigan Artist Award (both in 1993). Information on her work is included in *Contemporary Authors Autobiography Series,* vol. 23, *Oxford Companion to African American Literature, Dictionary of Literary Biography: Afro-American Writers, 1940–1955,* vol. 76, and other resources.

She is professor emeritus at Eastern Michigan University and publisher and editor of Lotus Press, which sponsors the annual Naomi Long Madgett Poetry Award, now in its seventh year.

Packrat

My trouble is
I always try to save
everything

old clocks and calendars
expired words buried
in open graves

But hoarded grains of sand
keep shifting as rivers
redefine boundaries and seasons

Lengths of old string
rolled into neat balls
neither measure nor bind

nor do shelves laden with rancid sweets
preserve
what ants continually nibble away

Love should be eaten
while it is ripe
and then the pits discarded

Lord give me at last
one cracked bowl holding
absolutely nothing

On Corcovado Mountain

High above the sands
of Rio, clouds veil
the impassive face

of the Redeemer.
Momentarily
pale sunlight steals through

seeking refuge in
folds of the stiffly
fluted skirt. Below

in deeper shadows,
in crevices of
precarious hills

crouch faceless squalid
children whom those out
stretched arms will never
hold, never redeem.

Reluctant Light

IN MEMORY OF MAUDE S. LONG

Mother, I didn't mean to slight you but
it wasn't you that I adored.
You hid your energy in shadows
and I was dazzled by the sun.

I idolized the one whose voice soared to prophetic heights,
whose words rejuvenated epics of the ages. Some fine June Sundays,
slender and magnificent in morning coat, he would electrify the pulpit
with eloquent pronouncements of doom and glory so divine
the very gates of heaven seemed to part, bathing the atmosphere in
    crystal light.
Seeking his favor, I rehearsed raising my hand like his in benediction,
earning the childhood name of Preacher, shortened in time to Preat.

You gave us daily sustenance but there was never
a choir's fanfare or the soulbeat of the mighty to grant applause.
You baked the bread for which we seldom thanked you,
canned pears for winter and mended Depression-weary clothes,
scrubbing sheets on a washboard, humming hymns to lift your sagging
    spirit,
and cultivating beauty in endless flower pots.
The summer when he toured the streets of ancient Palestine and Rome,
you consoled yourself by painting pictures of the Appian Way
using the kitchen table for an easel.

You coached me in my homework, rejoiced
in my small triumphs and prepared me to confront the enemy,
tapping your umbrella against my fifth grade teacher's desk
to punctuate your firm demand for justice. I didn't recognize
your subtle power that led me through blind, airless caves,
your quiet elegance that taught me dignity—nor could I know
the wind that bore *him* high into the sunlight
emanated from your breath. I didn't want your journey,
rebelled against your sober ways.

But I have walked through my own shadows and, like you,
transcended glitter. I have learned
that I am source and substance of a different kind of light.

Now when they say I look like you and tell me
that I have deepened to your wisdom, softened
to your easy grace, I claim my place with honor
in that court of dusky queens whose strength and beauty
invented suns that others only borrow. And Mother,
I am glad to be your child.

"The Sun Do Move"

Who wouldn't believe,
who wouldn't,
who wouldn't believe?

Camp meeting outside
the city limits.
Corn-high, the yellow wave
of faith, gushing
on his word.

And God said. . . .
> *Preach it, brotha!*
The Good Book reads. . . .
> *Yes, it do, Lawd, it do!*
Day climbing over the southeast
corner of the earth,
grasping for the truth.
> *Tell it, John Jasper,*
> *Hallelujah!*
All day long, all Sunday afternoon
the fields outside of Richmond rocking.

Sun melting down like lard
on the griddle of the world,
the hungry square of earth swallowing
it up again.
> *Come, Jesus!*

Who wouldn't believe,
who wouldn't, who
wouldn't believe!

Note: John Jasper (1812–1893 or 1901), a former slave, accepted the entire Bible literally and, through exhaustive study, was able to "prove" from Scripture the mobility of the sun and the flatness of the earth. His most famous sermon, "The Sun Do Move and the Earth Am Square," drew crowds of worshipers to his church in Richmond, Va., as well as to all-day camp meetings in the country. So thorough was his research, so convincing his sincerity and powerful his oratory that even those who knew better were convinced, even if only momentarily, of the authenticity of his claim.

Renewal

June is forever and forever returning.
Howling headlines will not prevent it.
Statistics cannot deny that which will be.

In my springtime heart I know that earth
will have its way. October, that old faker,
coloring its leaves in deceptive gaiety,

all the time meaning brittleness and brown
death, doesn't fool me. December's
snowflakes and gossamer enticements, hiding

sludge and dirt under the wings of Christmas
angels, can't forever deceive. I know
what I know. There is something in the nature

of things that is assuring, that tells me the people
emerging from their dark lives to front porches
and sunlight when the warm days come

know the secret the universe sometimes tries
to conceal. Life forever rejuvenates
itself. Whatever else happens, life lives.

Peter Markus

Peter Markus is a lifelong resident of Michigan. His poems have been published in *Third Coast*, *Black Warrior Review*, and *Quarterly West*. He was the recipient of a 1998–99 Creative Artist Award from ArtServe Michigan. He is the writer-in-residence at three Detroit Public Schools. He lives in Detroit.

Brothers

I'll give you this much, brother: you're nothing
if not punctual. When two a.m. bar time rolls
into town and that bittersweet mother of a barkeep
drawls in a voice that sounds like one of your ex-
lovers', "It's time you got on home," you drag
your boot heels over to the pay phone, punch
the numbers I wrote on the palm of your hand
one night last summer when the stitches criss-
crossing your wrist pricked me like the whiskers
on those blue-skinned catfish we used to catch
by the bucketful off the banks of the Detroit River,
our then unblemished hands bloodstained with stink
bait (back when *marriage* and *divorce* and *alcoholic*
were words only our parents sometimes whispered
out of earshot, hissed between clenched teeth),
and you sing me another whiskey-twisted version
of the same old song and dance, a song our fathers
sang on those graveyard mornings thirty years ago
after working the midnight shift at Great Lakes Steel.
They could've or should've been brothers, our mothers
liked to say, the way they drank, shot for shot, the way
they romped around town with ring-tailed metal shavings
dangling from yellow hard-hats. But now, my old man,
your old man, they don't even talk, let alone drink together.
Though you and I, yeah, brother, we still talk, and drink,
and shoot a cool game of stick, and the drunk-struck singers
our fathers used to croon to, slurred words whiskey-sung
—Hank Williams, Waylon Jennings, Johnny Cash—
still have a last best place to call home on jukeboxes
plugged in along West Jefferson, up and down Dix Highway,
a stretch of the county some folks call Kin-Taylor-tucky.
At first I would always ask, where are you calling from,
but now I can tell by the six-string slide of lap-steel
guitars, the two-stepping static in the back. Tonight
it's The Bottoms-Up bar down in River Rouge, a town
not too far from where we both got married, not too long

Peter Markus ⌣ 165

ago, but now you sleep with different women on different
nights of the week, while your wife has checked out west
to Montana, maybe, though you don't know exactly where.
I wonder if Hank Williams knew what he was singing
when he first strummed that open G-chord and hummed
the opening verse of "I'm So Lonesome I Could Cry."
I've often wondered what you'd do if I handed over
my out-of-tune acoustic guitar. I've got a bad feeling
you'd beat on it with the busted knuckles of your fist
as if it were your first-born bastard son. Our fathers
had hands that resembled junkyard steel, scrapped cars
gnarled and smudged with blood from drunken head-on
collisions on backstreets slickened with oil and rain,
sirens bleeding the sky red, mangled bodies dragged
already dead from metal our fathers might've made.
Now, when the call comes in the middle of the night,
I don't wake up, shaking, and think something's gone
wrong. Instead, I sit up in bed, and reach for the light.
And when I hear your voice singing out from the end
of the line, I go outside into the night, and I follow
my headlights until you step out of the darkness
like a ghost, or like the brother that I never knew.

Light

When he wasn't working, on his days off, his father liked to spend his day outside, in the shingle-bricked, single-car garage, tinkering with his '52 Chevy Bel Air: a stoop-roofed, two-toned junker he bought off a drunk buddy of his, a fellow hot metal man by the name of Lester Litwaski, for a fifth of whiskey and a scrunched-up dollar bill. There were days when his father wouldn't take five minutes to come into the house to eat a hot lunch. Days like these his mother'd send him outside into the garage with a cold corned beef sandwich and an apple, and his father'd stop working only long enough to wolf down this food, his hands gloved with grease and dust, before ducking back under the Chevy's jacked-up back-axle. Sometimes his father would fiddle around past midnight, his bent-over body half-swallowed by the open mouth of the hood, his stubby, blood-crusted fingers guided by the halogen glow of a single bare light-bulb hanging down, like a cartoon thought, above his hunch-backed silhouette. Sometimes he would stay up late and watch his father's shadow stretch like a yawn across the walls of the garage. And in the darkness of his room he would sit, silently, on the edge of the bed, by the window, and wait for that moment when his father raised up his hand, as if he were waving, as if he were saying good-bye, and turned off the light.

Black Light

For years he had heard his father talk about work, about carbon boils, tap holes, skulls of frozen steel. And he had spent many nights lying in bed awake, nights his father worked the graveyard shift, wondering what it all meant, as if the mill, and the life that went on inside it, was a part of some other world: a world he and his mother did not belong to. But one day all of this changed. One day he decided to ask his father if he could come inside, if he could go with his father to work, to see what it was like. And his father said he didn't see why not, though he'd have to clear it first with the plant manager, a tie- and-shirt type of guy by the name of Russell Prescott. Which he did. And a date was set for that following Monday. And so, instead of getting ready to go to bed like he usually did at eleven o'clock, listening to the final innings of the Detroit Tiger game, the voice of Ernie Harwell drawling through the dime-sized speaker on his transistor radio, he found himself walking the quarter of a mile upriver with his father, step by step in the darkness of this mid-July night, the sky frosted fly-ash gray with a haze that hung over in the wake of the day's ninety-degree heat. His father didn't say anything the whole way there, though as they passed through the black-grated entry gates of Great Lakes Steel, he pushed his hand down into his front trouser pocket and pulled out two tiny tablets of salt: white like plain aspirin. "You think it's hot out here," his father warned. "Just wait until we get inside." And then his father dropped the pills into his hand. And it was true. Inside, the heat made it hard for him to breathe. The hot metal was so bright, it was so black with light, he could barely stand to watch as it drained from the blast furnace down to the thermo ladle waiting below. He closed his eyes, held in his breath. But still he could see the sudden flash of molten sparks showering down, could taste the burn of cooked limestone slag, could feel the callused hand of his father reaching out towards him, taking hold of him, turning him away from the light.

On Becoming a Bird

One day he decides that he wants to be a bird. Not a firefighter or an astronaut or a doctor or even a nurse. But a bird! That's nice, honey, his mother tells him. Now go watch TV. But his father wants to know what kind of a bird. The boy gnaws on his bottom lip. What kind of a bird? Yeah, you know, his father replies. A robin? A sparrow? A blackbird? A crow? The boy cocks his head off to the side. He looks up at the ceiling and believes it's the sky. After a while he turns back to his father and says, Dad, I've made up my mind. A pigeon. That's the bird I want to be. His father considers the boy's decision. Whispers the word, *pigeon*. Pauses. Shrugs. Hawks his brow. A pigeon, he figures, is a classic, blue-collar bird. Nothing fancy. Not some sissy songbird. Okay, he tells his son. But wait here. He puts his hand on the boy's shoulder. Says: I got something to give to you. The boy looks on in silence as his father disappears into the kitchen. He hears the metallic click of his father's lunchbucket lid flipping open. When his father returns half a minute later, his right hand is clenched into a fist. Here, his father says. And opens his hand. The boy opens his eyes to find a palmful of breadcrumbs. He doesn't hesitate, he doesn't wait for others to join in. He lowers his head, as if in prayer, and begins to eat.

Photo by Mary Whalen

David Marlatt

David Marlatt lives in Richland, Michigan. His collection of poetry, *A Hog Slaughtering Woman*, was published by New Issues Press in 1996.

Horse Hair Mattress

I could never sleep
on the horse hair mattress
in the back bedroom of my aunt's house.
She carried me up the back steps afternoons
laying my wide child ears down
against the mattress ticking.
I could never sleep.
She told me
of Uncle Frank shearing
orange mane
from his matched chestnuts.
I rubbed my ear on the mattress
thinking only of Frank,
dirty hat on,
his own hair matted
against his scalp,
clipping handfuls of hair
with blunt-nosed
nickel-plated shears.
I knew he coiled the hair
in a burlap bag,
saved it
until there was enough
to fill a whole mattress,
but I could never sleep
on it. I kept thinking
of my aunt washing, soaking the mix
of mane and tail
in a galvanized tub
sudsed with the clear green
Superior cake soap Frank sold
in winter.
Spread on a sheet,

the mottled hairs reflected the sun.
I could never sleep
on the flattened hair
saved and packed tight
so many years.
I couldn't sleep
with all that mane
and tail hair blowing
over those horses'
necks and backs
from one side to the other
cutting furrows up
cutting furrows back.

Trout

I had to explain to her that she was as beautiful
as a trout. Not a bluegill but a trout
with brown spots finely dusted over her arms
and back. I had to explain to her that a trout was the best of fish.
Not the fish caught green over the side of a bridge
with its gasping gills, wide underslung mouth, and stomach
spewing out worm muck.
I swam with her, and I said she looked like a trout
drawn long and sleek out of a cold gravel stream. Too fine-lined
to be cut open, her own stomach, back, arms, thighs
tightly packed. Her long hair, neck, and chest
leaving the water with white skin showing off her spots
small and unseen
like on the belly of a trout,
brown against the underside of the fish, jerking
against the green grass of the bank.

Spring Thaw

Streams of rust
run off the broken hinges
nailed tight to the old man's shed,
waiting for the long dead smith in Cressy
to mend the halves.
There are other things too,
like hitch bolts and bicycle chains,
that put back together could always be used for something.
But the smith's dead,
buried up on the graveled hillside in Cressy,
surrounded by twisted shafts,
peened and drawn to hundreds of sharp points
around that untillable hillside.
He's dead and he's been dead
and so is just about everybody else
who ever brought a horse to be shod
or logging chain to be relinked.
But still the old man saves everything in bundles,
in boxes, in crates, and barrels,
for another depression, another life,
for his son in Chicago to turn the burdock and sumac sprouts
in the spring.
But the boy's had enough summers
of twine burns behind a stationary baler,
and trips to the elevator scoop-shoveling corn
into the spiraling auger of its bottomless grate.
He'll never be back.
The cans pile up outside the rotting threshold
in bulging burlap bags.
The old man stuffs rags in broken window panes.
The whole place will burn one morning
sealing the bargain in a handshake of flame
while he's on his knees
lighting the stove.

Dahlias

Dahlias, we planted dahlias, digging a trench around the house.
Summers, my mother planted giant dahlias. The tubers were a gift
overflowing the brown paper bag onto the ground
under the apple trees. The blossoms were pink
and white, growing almost five inches
in diameter, and I wanted to climb
into the center and go to sleep in the curve of
one petal growing from the yellow star center.
I asked my mother to plant a blue dahlia
like the dahlia in the Raymond Chandler movie. She said
there was no such thing.
The dahlias bloomed. The fall bloomed with dahlias
along the cracked foundation.
The next year we had so many dahlias my father and I
planted them in a row
as long as the sweetcorn in the garden. And the dahlias
still came multiplying better than potatoes. If only dahlias
could be eaten. We stacked crates, winters,
in my aunt's cellar clear to the ceiling in two rows
never letting them freeze in the ground.
William Bendix went insane in Chandler's movie watching
a woman pull petals from a blue dahlia. His steel-plated skull
throbbed at the sight of the falling dahlia
petals on the glass counter reflecting the rising
dahlia petals. My aunt hated them in her cellar
adding more dirt and dahlia rot to her dirt floor.
The year my father died, we let the tubers freeze in the ground.
Leftover sprouts dried to knotted wood, or
softened, hanging through the bottom slats
of the crates. My mother would not spade a hole
or break dahlia clumps sprouted that spring. She wouldn't
stake a dahlia stalk too overgrown to stand on its own
in sandy ground that spring without my father,
a spring without dahlias.

A Hog Slaughtering Woman

1

When Frances Woodburry ran her dark Falcon sedan
head into our loose hog, it was a hot day not given
to idle talk or the shuffling of papers.

2

Frank moved from his down print in the tapestry chair
more excited than when the piano tuner came
wobbling a wrench and spreading a hand to strike

3

intervals that echoed, attenuated seamlessly through
the ductwork and pipes, through the screen door
all over the yard.

4

My mother was not sorry, save seeing
blood puddled under the burr oak, acorns
washed in the long wind-turned grass.

5

I had never seen Frank's blackened hams hanging in the cellar must,
high to the floor joist from a spike,
tied, bound by several twists of twine.
His curing days of rubbing in salt and smoking were over.

6

If he had planned the afternoon, it would not have been as good,
a heavy woman from up the road bending to butcher
a hog in the side yard, the concave chrome of a Falcon's bumper,

7

an old man sharpening and resharpening knives
against the bone, against the sound of oil and stone.

Photo by Betsy Ramsey

Gail Martin

Gail Martin was born in Flint, Michigan, in 1952. Her recent work appears in
Poetry Northwest and *Sonora Review*. She was the 1999 first place winner of
the National Poet Hunt sponsored by the *MacGuffin*. She currently lives in
Kalamazoo with her husband and three daughters.

The Thing He Regretted

FOR SUN YAOTING, THE LAST EUNUCH OF THE LAST EMPEROR, 1902–1996

1

In your gray city
you need a dose
of red, in your cold
city, teeth acquire
a grittiness that
is hard to brush away.
Is it from the soft coal you burn?
The loess dust from the Gobi
blowing in unchecked from
Mongolia? You will not say.

2

I meet a Californian
marketing pharmaceuticals
for Belgium. He tells me
that your country is not
inscrutable. That there is much
more color on the street
than 15 years ago. His wife
raids Mass for Filipina girls
who know how to keep
a house clean. He plays
jazz for me in his home on Embassy
Row and tells me how amusing
it is to watch the rush-rush
long noses negotiate with
the Chinese, who take the longer
view. (*If the tree does not*
bear fruit in this lifetime, maybe
in the next.)

3

In your forbidden city, I see
a marble square where hot
chili sauce and a small
curved knife met your

three precious,
the surgeon at the
gate who sold you back
your own genitals
in a jar. I think of you,
your high voice,
your soft body,
carrying your jar,
banking on the fullness
of manhood in the next life.

4

A woman squats
beside a dirt road.
She holds a machete
and whacks
designs into small pineapples,
intricate as cloisonné.
Around her are bundles
of wet greens she is selling,
three white ducks still as snow piles.
Are they drugged? Is it true
their legs are bound or removed?
You do not say.

5

We hand bright jelly-beans
to black-haired children
in red jackets. We watch
them throw the candy
hard against the cement steps,
like cherry bombs, or small firecrackers,
waiting for the explosion.

6

Your felt-covered feet bring
rice and chopsticks to our table
for breakfast. (We have sent back
the duck's feet, and their bills.)

7

We tour a cloisonné factory.
Here women work
in cold rooms, on concrete floors.
It is gray, the work is tedious.
Small women
piece in entire patterns
with delicate instruments,
smiling into their hands.

8

In your forbidden city,
I see gilded water containers
the size of small limousines,
a hedge against fire,
incense burners as large as
shacks, shaped like cranes,
dragons, tortoises.
You have spent 94 years
in the hall of abstinence.

9

At dawn the old men come
to the bird market.
Their brown hands are tender
and gnarled as banyan trees.
They hold ornate cages,
are out walking their birds!
Our guide makes fun of them.
"Just old men and their games," she says.
The men open cellophane bags full
of small green grasshoppers and dip them
in honey for the birds. They stroke
the throat of each bird to sweeten his song.
In my mind, I see a procession of eunuchs
ending with you. They are walking the hall
of emperor's long life. The hall of three purities.
They are diving deep underwater to hang
small fish or a precious jewel on the emperor's hook.

10

I keep returning to you.
I roll your plumpness
over in my mind until
you become a buddha
when you are merely a man.
I roll you around like a hard
candy melting in my mouth.
Like the harmony balls
that I bought as gifts in your
country. They are steel
and iridescent, are said
to prevent loss of memory.
They are cold
and my palms do not warm them.
I rotate them in my hand. Just
two balls, once the treasure
of Baoding, now hollow,
now chiming in low tones.

Woman of Wood

Kindling so delicate
your heart cracks open
as you gather it
into your arms.
Georgia fatwood, shiny
and dry, panting
for flame, ready to give
it all up to smoke. Finally,
the seasoned log of apple,
a lady's scent. Can you see
my eyes in flame?
Over time, I've been felled,
bucked, skidded and hauled.
Sorted and graded by men
with big appetites, split
up the middle with buzzsaws.
And still I'm the pine knot torch

carried by search parties
when you lose your child,
the bed carved of hard maple
where you breathe your
last furry breath, the plumb
mast of this ship sailing
toward an unmapped continent.

Woman of Water

You were wise, clinging
to the shore, the side
of the lost vessel. You
should be afraid. Oh, sure,
I douse barn fires,
passed in buckets
from neighbor to
neighbor as they stand
in their foolish nightshirts.
I'll sweeten the dirt
of your June garden.
But I'm moody,
move from trickle
to gush in the time it takes
a tear, a needle
of rain to drop.
Ask the fishermen
who've encountered me
off Newfoundland
in November, when my freak
seas are so lush with plankton
that I swallow the light, where
my rogue waves are mistaken
for the moon.
Make no mistake;
your buoyancy is not
flight. I'll take your weight
away, and then your breath.

Photo by Lisa Powers

Joseph Matuzak

Joe Matuzak is author of one book of poetry, *Eating Fire* (Ridgeway Press, 2000), and his poetry, fiction, and essays have appeared in the *Georgia Review, Kansas Quarterly, Passages North, Controlled Burn,* and other magazines and anthologies. He is currently director of Arts Wire, a program of the New York Foundation for the Arts. His writing has received a Creative Artists Award and Hopwood Awards from the University of Michigan.

Rust

Doorbell, quick rustling, and a basket
moored to top step with dismal note:
"Please look after my child, please,
care and nurture, build, make strong."
Christ! I thought, what a city, what a world,
then peeled back the basket's grayed linen cover.

Inside lay only piles of silvery bolts and brassy pins,
Heaps of screws with stripped threads, scruff and slivers,
little odd grinds of steel, and bent aluminum bars.
Another crank, another joke, something for the trash heap.
But as I closed my door, there floated out a whimper,
small, like far off radio, or neighbor's muffled telephone.
I searched across the yard, couldn't find the source,
but still that crying remained, coming from the basket,
vibrating, sputtering like a mis-fed engine.

No directions, so I assembled pieces the best I could.
When finished I had a baby, made of all these odd parts,
but kicking and gurgling like any other, grasping
with metal hand and shiny eyes to take in all the world.
So I reared that child as my own, clothed and fed it,
cleaned and taught. When time came the child went to school,
was taunted for its differences, cried greasy tears,
and my fears were those of any parent.

A metal child grows in dangerous ways:
stray dents and quick patches, magnetism and soldering.
Many times the child returned home late,
and attached I'd see another dingy bolt or loose hinge,
some worrisome spike or blinking contradictory panel,
and I would tighten and sand, polish, oil and scrape,
until the child would scream, no, I like it just the way it is.
I'd hear that damned hinge squawk and squeak all night,
and the child would rock itself, jitter and howl with delight.

Time, time, time. I now feel myself turning to metal;
this voice raspy with the grind of worn parts, back a string of frozen
    flanges.

What mother, what father gave up this child to me?
What kind of city stamps impressions on it like a factory?
Outside it is raining, a downpour that goes on forever.
The child I assembled rusts in spite of my love.

Poaching with Darby and Happy Harry

The boat is borrowed,
so no loss if seized,
as it follows low tide out
on this moonless night.
Darby's arms, at sixty-five,
are rock tight from a
lifetime of stealth,
and he slides the oars
as if the water were
butter, churning no
tell-tale splashes
that might alert
the game wardens.
I stand on shore
and hold one end of the net
again, so if someone's
caught, it's me, and
then in the black stale
breath of the night
the tide changes and
the first fish arrows
panic-stricken into
the net. Every
strum of his tail
travels like a chord up
the sinew to play this
song: the business of
poaching is killing.

Eating Fire

I first started eating fire for money,
quick sips of butane and bottled beer,
small bets in the bar with drunks,
but then I grew
to love the taste, the raw
and acrid burn as it extinguishes.

Every day I chew the fruits
of the earth, fill myself with
water and air to stay alive,
but it is fire that stokes the engine,
fire that is the hamster on the wheel,
fire that brings me closer
to the ash I will become.

I have saturated my body
with the honeyed smell
of arson, sweet and
volatile as religious rumor,
holy cool tongues dancing
like lozenges made of fireflies.

(When Moses first saw
the burning bush
he ran away
driven not by fear but desire,
sweet tremor,
and when he returned
reached his hand
into the inferno and began
to pluck and then consume
the fiery berries. Branch
by flaming branch he ate the
rest, and smoldered with
the unnamable. When he tried
to describe the texture,
everything came out as law.)

The Size of Heaven

Less than one by one square inch,
it sports the rough grain of a sea wall pitted
by hand with adz then sanded with centuries
of salt wind and ocean thrown from winter storms
that gallop direct across the polar cap
from Siberia. As you watch, it blossoms,
exploding with variegated greens and brown pollen motes
that throb and swirl like a fresh poured glass of black and tan,
a slow insect species pas de deux
of yellow bees and fireflies. It pulses, thrums
with murmured voices brimming candles
and sedatives. You want it added to your drink.

From within, it stretches always just a little further
than can be traveled any given day, resetting boundaries
with semantic tricks of light that can't be resolved
or quite exactly defined while happening,
a Mobius strip of history where on one side
every inch of the sacred ground has been inhabited
by the same family for centuries,
and on the other each individual footstep sinks
into lush grass that's never been glimpsed by anyone.

Here is the black hole of distance become sugar cube for your tea.
Here is time compressed to tight bright lips snicking
like mirthful switchblades, a sweet threat
to slice the horizon full of petal smiles and laughter.
You must watch continuously, as it wickedly undulates its hips.

What's that? By some mistake you loosened your grip,
left it an accidental instant on table or
in the china saucer while you refilled your cup?
When you did that the edges smoothed.
It curled tight into a fiery glass eyeball and rolled off
like a marble in search of a circle.
It found someone who was looking, and leapt like a kitten
toward their face. It might be there, looking back at you

from your neighbor, your daughter, your dog. You have
to find it. You have to fog it with your breath.
It is the worst addiction you can imagine.

"I with no rights in the matter"

For years you proclaimed it wasn't you he hit,
that was another person, it wasn't you,
couldn't have been, you wouldn't allow it.
You start, pounded from sleep, and again those blows
creep through carefully constructed brick-like walls
like basement moisture into the carpeted present,
huge cartoon kapows and kablooeys,
thrown from this man long gone.

All these years and I've rarely raised my voice,
most certainly never my hand to you,
but that serves only as balm to deep wounds,
whispers idleness to my dreams,
does not make my name or face
a moon to illumine your landscape.

I am a worker at Chernobyl, cleaning, cleaning,
and while the task is done with pleasure and hope,
slowly I'm irradiated into sterility.
Everything becomes computerized: Intent. Interpretation.
Evaluation. Reconfiguration. Only then, action.
House of mirrors, refracting and distorting.
Through two decades he has never stopped striking
at our life, poisoning every sentence or gesture
lest it be received by you with dread.

I am a sea wall. I am a fire department. I am a kitchen rag.
I am everything but the one who has marked you so deeply
you want most a dream that is neutral,
sleep without disturbance, without a man who capsizes
it in any way. For me, who wants to be the focus
of your nights, what kind of dream is that?
It is terrible to know we can be stained
more brightly by fear than by love.

Photo by Rhys Van Demark

Kathleen McGookey

Kathleen McGookey was born in Grand Rapids in 1967 and has lived in Michigan all her life, except for one year when she lived in Paris. Her poems have appeared or are forthcoming in the *Bellingham Review, Boston Review, Cimarron Review, Epoch, Field,* the *Journal,* the *Laurel Review,* the *Missouri Review, Poetry East, Quarter after Eight, Quarterly West, Seneca Review,* and *Verse.* Her first collection, *Whatever Shines,* will be published by New Rivers Press in 2001. She is finishing her PhD at Western Michigan University.

Honeymoon

The animals are sick with love. A white dog
walks the beach like a shadow. A blue heron perches
on the dock, its long neck one deep loop.
Someone was eating roses and reading

love letters while the sea turtles ate out of our hands.
I want the heron to stay. It could have good news.
I could be what it wants. You have to put your face
in the water and breathe, the woman says,

breathe, and the bubbles grow until they surface,
where I float with the jellyfish, where I'll catch them.
I'm sorry I feel this way. There's a spider
on the towel I've just used to dry my hair.

The string quartet followed them in the garden,
the sun shining and all the boats on the lake
gathered out front, and happily,
no one fell into the cake. Acres of sunflowers

bent their bright heads to the bride.
One must surface slowly for all kinds of reasons.
Your lungs could explode. Look,
I can't tell you what's wrong,

it's very loud and the air rattles my mask
like too much rain. I am crying with a stranger.
She asks, "Are you doing it for him?"
I am sick on the beach on a white towel, I am sick

and doing it for him, the animals are sick,
and the parrotfish swim close because I want them.
Why are the beaches deserted and the restaurants empty,
why can no one serve us what we want,

a simple sweet piece of key lime pie?
Animals stamped on silver coins.
It's not too late to ask the blue heron to stay,
to drop what we can't carry, but listen,

I'm not going to beg. There are no love letters on the reef.
When it rains, we run to the covered part of the boat:
everything begins here, including bad weather. Here money
is no object, and we pay and pay.

Poem for My Mother,

who said, I'll bet you can put *that* in a poem. Here are the guests
throwing water balloons at my wedding and later, Clarence shooting his
rifle at water snakes. Not at my wedding, but across the lake. Two
houses down, Jack shoots raccoons from his living room couch; think
what you will but it's quite a nice neighborhood. Here I am riding in the
backseat with my mother's old ladies; Margaret Lubbers fell asleep on
me and I thought she might have died. Most of all, here I am alone at a
party for high school friends, one so fat now she might be mistaken for
pregnant though she owns a lovely firelit lakeside home. Because they
didn't hear the doorbell, I thought, I might not go in, I did my best.
Still, I sit by the hearth and clap for the engaged couple and think, a
house like this can't make you thin. Which is the truth. Which does
little to make me feel better, I am ashamed of my heart and still haven't
told about Diet Coke in crystal goblets and chatter and bone white hope
and panic when the person who spoke to me most went across the
room to wash dishes. Would they ever cut the cake? I can be rude on
the phone but not face to face. How about the weather, how about the
fishing up north? Look. The way I see it, if we get enough rain, we
could just drift away.

Block Party

Then voices. Then silence. Then the sky rumbled. Shivery light forked on the horizon. I mean lightning. Don't blink. I ran to set out my tin can. Then rain poured into the basement and washed all the cardboard boxes away. But now the sky is lit with clouds and patches of blue. No one's screaming. The doves dream on telephone wires, dreaming dove-dreams where all the hunters fall and rip their jeans and scramble home to change. The metal pails dream of brimming, overfilling and then the moment when it spills, water's brief life. Still, no one's screaming, such a messy word; it's awkward like *flailing*, or *failing*, when something's wrong no matter how carefully the evening was planned. Most events go on in the rain, though they'll have to rent a white tent and the doves that are released will bump into the ceiling. What were they dreaming of? Telephone wires, that's right, and the thousand thousand conversations rushing through their claws. Thick voices. Long pauses. Was that the baby screaming? No, just someone crying over sheets dried on the line, and the children who rode through them—look how the walls disappeared!—on tricycles. It wasn't planned or schemed; the sheets presented themselves, a sunny day, an expanse of green. Someone sold the dream of sun and kids on bikes, a block party where we all eat berries and cream. But they set up the tables in my grandparents' new garage, on account of the rain. Inside the rain's hush, the doves rustled their wings and practiced their soft calls. Calling here, here, here. Calling me.

Line from a Journal

FOR MY GRANDMOTHER

Thoroughly happy, making beds and washing dishes?
I don't believe you meant that, but maybe you are,
maybe, that newly married moment in 1935 as you sit writing
while your husband visits the men in his Benton Harbor office.
Maybe then, happy, so different from when you came home
to dishes after school (were you always doing dishes?),
the water cold and greasy, the fire dying, the black saucepan
you could barely lift.

You sit writing, half in and half out of the light,
making sense of your latest good fortune. Are you always a little afraid
it is a dream? Not only a dream of being warm, finally,
but of having enough: money, coal, new furniture and books,
no rain. A cool moon shines on your last night
as nurse's supervisor. Will you miss your job? Your name?
But still, this is no dream, you thought the ceremony real,
then the tall grass bows down as you drive to Traverse City.
Your silver ring etched with orange blossoms. Your brown suit
with lace at the throat. Fallen gold leaves are so thick you can't see
the ground. Stray dogs run behind the car, happy in their wild eyes.
Rain, and then your car next on the terrible scene: you place
your husband's clean handkerchief over the face,
apply pressure to the chest. It is terrible, the only crash
you've seen right after. You bite your own cheek raw.

At home, your dogs in their cages sniff and groan.
Is night lonely without him, his letters arriving
like too much light, strong sweets? You watch the jays
and the lake and the flames. You bend over your cookbook, determined
to poach an egg and set a table correctly. You write,
and watch the moths fly to the light.

Last Night, an Owl

called its grief into the dark, over and over.
The mourning doves only cooed, stupid enough to stay
in the road. Too late, boats come in from the lake.
It could end here, my half-constructed grief
for the girl I might have been, dressed smartly,
speaking another language in a cafe.
Desire of my own making hangs around me: I share an ice cream,
lick by lick, in front of the subway station; I go off
with strangers near the quiet fountains slimy with moss.
Someone is breathing outside my window.
It's as if I'd never left, or wanted to,
this strange cycle: a wedding, a body other than mine,
a warm house, a dog.

We could see the owl in its nest, growing. But the leaves came
and we forgot it there, flying and calling at night, calling itself
into my sleep where someone was giving me a gift.
But here are two seagulls bothering the loon,
here is the dog with a dead rabbit in her mouth. Here are my mother
and grandmother still in their bodies with the child reaching
for the mirror.

It may sound crazy but last week I interviewed a woman
and halfway through, thought I *was* her, watching myself talk.
I am waiting for a day where the light is in the sky before I am,
and pours itself into me. I can't look.
I am not singing. I am not confusing the mist over the lake
and the road with the light I am looking for, the absolute word.
Finally, enough fireflies and sleep. A small ache.

Photo by Robert Turney

Judith Minty

Judith Minty is the author of four full-length poetry collections and three chapbooks. Her first book, *Lake Songs and Other Fears,* was recipient of the United States Award of the International Poetry Forum in 1973. Her most recent book is *Walking with the Bear: New and Selected Poems* (2000). She has taught at several colleges and universities in the United States, most recently Humboldt State University in Arcata, California, where she directed the creative writing program. She also received the 1998 Mark Twain Award for Distinguished Contributions to Midwestern Literature from the Society for the Study of Midwestern Literature. Minty lives along the Lake Michigan shoreline with her husband and a yellow dog named River.

Deer at the Door

What drew them up the hill, away
from sheltering pines, overgrown sumac, everything
in leaf now that summer's nearly here?
Was it light inside this little house,
our soft conversation, our attention
to the roast, the salad, before us?
What is it they saw, standing by the window,
their gentle heads raised, then browsing
again in the grass? Was it our shadows
bent over our plates, our acceptance
of what we have, what we are,
as the slow weight of day began to leave?
—I remember the beginning of a moment:
the sparrow's throat opening, the dog
rising from her place on the rug, me standing, you
looking up, the song starting, the dog and I
crossing the room, my hand on the door,
the smiles on our faces, the song on its last notes,
everything in harmony for a few beats of the heart.
Then the door opened
and their heads lifted, the air turned still.
I heard the rustle of grass, saw their white tails flash
as they darted awkwardly down the hill,
and dusk came on like the closing of an eye.

At Manitoulin

North Channel, Canada

The summer I sailed among islands,
rowdy teenagers came to the government wharf
where I'd tied for the night. I shouldn't have been
on reservation land and was afraid
they might cut my lines, set me adrift in the starless dark.
"Please," I called, standing at the open hatchway, "can you
not be so noisy? I'm trying to sleep."
In the silence, eyes of cigarettes glowed.
—At dawn, I gathered empty bottles left against the pilings.

It was noon when the Indian boy came on his pony,
its hooves clattering over the dock's rough timbers.
Neither of them had been this close to a sailboat, and the horse
shied when I came onto the deck.
The boy peered into the cabin for a long time before he
climbed down, then he touched the gimballed stove,
the instruments on the chart table, he trailed his finger
over the fences that held my books in their shelves.

He sat on the edge of a berth and drank juice I poured,
and told how the pony had studied its face
in the dusty window of his grandpa's shed
until it fell in love with its own image. He said
he'd like to go to school on the mainland,
maybe travel to the States when he grew up.
Before I set sail, I gave the horse two carrots,
the boy helped me cast off. When I got to open water,
I looked back at the two of them, standing at the end
of the dock—the boy's arm around the pony's neck,
the pony whispering in his ear.

The Language of Whales

Car wipers clearing a path through mist,
I come to where the beached whale
lies rotting at the shoreline.
Last night it was the strum of harps.
Before that, cellos. Today, a chorus singing.
Past a barrier of rock and shallows,
beyond the roll and curl of surf,
they rise and fall, they call him home.

All winter I waited at my window,
walked the cliff for the miracle of seeing
spout or breech or trail of bubbles.
I imagined their bodies light as clouds
gliding over, slipping under, each other.
Last year, from a boat, I watched
three cross our bow—eye and back, then fluke.
I heard them sigh as they breathed in air.

Once, at the Ocean Grove Bar, I met
an old whaler mourning his youth.
"We'd get between the calf and cow
and spear the youngster first," he said.
"The mother was easy after that."
—Don't stop here, don't climb the dune, don't look
at that obscene word someone carved in his flesh.
"Come," they sing across the waves.

When my Cherokee friend was a boy in Oklahoma
a whale was hauled through on a train.
He remembers the crowd at the station, his mother
holding his hand, the dust on his shoes,
the summer heat, the huge shadow
like a felled tree on the flatbed.
He remembers the voices calling—all that way.

October Light

1. Driving

Driving past blur of fencepost,
past cornstalks bleached and bent,
past fallow fields and grasses dying on the shoulder,
lost in the business of highway, of getting
from point to circled map-point, towns
rolling by like old newsreels,
the eye's pupil narrows, won't open
its tiny focus or let the hungry heart expand
until the car stops at the pond.
Here, sun pierces the brilliant sky,
weave of color in the hills,
pattern of green and gold and scarlet,
fleck of mauve. Here, blood seeps
down branch and trunk to yellow
already scattered on the bank, to reflection
where mind sees at last
what heart needs, sees water
open its mouth and swallow all this brilliance.

2. In Town

Up Maple Street, over on Elm,
down Locust near the Trinity Union Church,
around corners, near fenceposts,
in sunlight's blaze and leaf-turn,
this town prepares for spirits.
Skeletons leap from parlor windows, pumpkins
spill down drives, witches' brooms
and sheaves of husks stand sentinel at stairs.
On white-washed porches, rag-stuffed aged
accept the wind in chairs that rattle as they rock.
This town is old, history was born here—
land was cleared, a war was fought,
gossip stretches back for generations.
At dusk, these robed and melon-headed ghosts,
tied now and hanging from the maples,
will dance and beckon to the cemetery,
calling home the rest of it.

3. Home

Traveling from workplace, from meeting room,
from neighboring town or store or mall,
along roads on fire with sumac and sugar maple,
the heart smolders in a passion of oak.
Past yellow poplar and beech, past trembling birch,
past staccato of black gum by the orchard, past
blaze of blueberry bush and humming meadow grass.
At last, up the winding two-track, key already turned
to unlock the inner life, house inside these golden ash trees,
secret veins and bones of floor and wall and roof.
Climbing the stairs, opening the door, entering
this heat—this light—that leans willingly into winter.

Photo by D. C. Goings

Thylias Moss

Thylias Moss is the author of, most recently, *Tale of a Sky-Blue Dress*, a memoir published in 1998 by Avon Books, *Last Chance for the Tarzan Holler*, her sixth collection of poetry, published by Persea Books in 1998, and *I Want to Be*, a book for children from Dial Books for Young Readers. Among her many awards and prizes are a MacArthur Fellowship, a Guggenheim Fellowship, a Whiting Writer's Award, the Witter Bynner Prize, the National Poetry Series Open Competition, the Dewar's Profiles Performance Artist Award, and a Pushcart Prize. Her work has appeared in six volumes of the *Best American Poetry* annual series, including the 1998 edition, and the *Best of the Best* edition, also published in 1998. *Pyramid of Bone*, her second volume of poetry, was short-listed for the National Book Critics Circle Award. She teaches at the University of Michigan and lives in Ann Arbor with her husband and two sons.

The Limitation of Beautiful Recipes

FOR DEIRDRE

With the silver ladle that belongs
to both of our families alternating years

we take from under the rose bush
as much dirt as the punch bowl will hold, then add:

talcum, water, Old Spice, Avon's Persian Wood,
Eight O'clock Coffee, cold cream, Comet, Miracle Whip,
pureed clams, salt, lemon juice, and grated pink Camay,
everything on hand in two households except

blessed assurance though we hum as we stir it smooth,
spoon it into Dixie cups, rush to the front yard yelling:

Cleopatra's Formula without which she was no queen.
Take our word; we're both hundreds of years old, experts
in the business; just look, feast your eyes
on what's yours for 25¢; only 25¢!

Jimmy is first to let us coat his face, and we aren't ready
to kiss him though I could push Deirdre's mouth on his
as she avoids his eyes. In a week we are rich so we
make a cake and bake Bosco into chocolate bars and

chocolate blotches all over the walls and ceiling, stunned
by the limitation of beautiful recipes.

Even so we take our formula to one of our mothers
who does not notice the proximity of cure so busy is she
pulling out her hair. We stare at piles of thin wire

wanting to believe in the freedom and power
dismantling can mean
for a woman who tells us in a voice almost singing

that someone we know is gone, hair, hope, and all.
Taken by bullets to where we are heading, little girls
who defer to wolves and shotguns

in the name of helping our mothers
take the ladle and covered casseroles into the house
where blood dried dark as chocolate, and where morning's

first sounds are wails that become melodic and perfect
as our mothers bow down, the hair of one
tumbling over three shoulders.

The Right Empowerment of Light

In the right empowerment of light, pictures taken
are so well washed I get 4 x 6-inch rectangles
of light's domination.

In a photo of rural Japanese radishes that light finishes
with translucence, vegetables become slender lanterns
destined to appear as specialty of the house, but how to serve
the light, how to slice it; how to bite it, swallow it
without the chest lighting up, ribs becoming frame
for a lamp shade?
In church you chew on His death; you don't sample
His infinity. What is the etiquette?

In the film about the infant emperor
the royal feces was collected in brass
jade and gold
and gave off light
in the kingdom so there was no opposition
to the production of milk by his wet nurse
for his lifetime that gave off light
in the beam of piss that in the sand
formed veins of gold.

I want to say it's radioactive: that last summer,
his sisters in the house first time in years,
I walked into the room rebellion with me
yet my father lit up, they said.

There is divine light.
There is also arrogance, the other
radiance.

A Hot Time in a Small Town

In this restaurant a plate of bluefish pâté
and matzos begin memorable meals.

The cracker is ridged, seems planked, an old wall
streaked sepia, very nearly black
in Tigrett, Tennessee

where it burned

into a matzo's twin. While waiting
for a Martha's Vineyard salad, I rebuild the church
with crackers, pâté as paste

as a flaming dessert arrives at another table where diners
are ready for a second magnum of champagne; every day
is an anniversary; every minute, a commemoration
so there is no reason to ever be sober

to excuse incendiaries who gave up the bottle,
threw alcohol at the church, spectacular reform

in flames themselves ordinary—there'd been fire in that church
many times, every Sunday and even at the Thursday
choir rehearsals. For years there'd been a fired-up congregation

so seething, neighborhoods they marched through ignited
no matter their intention; just as natural as summer.
There were hot links as active as telephone lines
whose poles mark the countryside as if the nation is helpless
without a crucifix every few yards; pity they are combustible

and that fire itself is holy, that its smoke merges with atmosphere,
that we breathe its residue, that when it is thick and black enough
to believe in, it betrays and chokes us; pity
that it is the vehicle that proves the coming of the Lord,
the establishment of his kingdom, his superiority because

fire that maintains him disfigures us; when we try to embrace
him; we find ourselves out on a limb burning. The meal

tastes divine, simply divine
and I eat it in the presence of a companion dark as scab,
as if skin burned off was replaced as he healed
with this total-body scab

under which he is pink as a pig, unclean at least
through Malachi.

In my left hand, a dash of Lot's wife; in my right, a mill
to freshly grind the devil; since fire is power
both the supreme good and supreme evil are entitled
to it; most of the time, what did it matter
who was in charge of Job? Both burnt him.

Photo by Mary Whalen

Julie Moulds

Poet Julie Moulds has battled non-Hodgkin's lymphoma for seven years, through remissions, recurrences, and a bone marrow transplant. Her first book of poems, *The Woman with a Cubed Head,* was published by New Issues Press in 1998. Her poems have appeared in *Cream City Review, New York Quarterly,* and *Quarterly West.*

Renoir's Bathers

What is it about women in water
that almost makes them part of the landscape?
Renoir's bathers, pink and mustard
and vaguely nippled; their ample thighs
rising from a purple river in a scene
centered by one brown tree. What is it
about women, painted by men,
that they become landscapes, creamy roses
in a garden? In another age,
when people could still sleep
with almost anyone, my sister and I dipped
ourselves naked in a Michigan lake, both of us,
still, miraculously, virgins.
I suppose some painter in that art colony
where Brenda washed dishes
could have captured us, like Renoir,
two flowers with leafy thighs and brown
daisy faces. Perhaps he would accent
our round hymens with petals. I want to be
the woman, with her brush, sitting in an oak
above a pond where twelve nude men are frolicking.
She is painting a landscape of men:
lying flat with grapes above their open mouths;
men, with buttocks turned towards her; men
with arms arched behind their long necks.
She would call it *The Dozen Adonae*. Pink
chrysanthemum men; dark, magnolia men;
legs spread; organs rising or fallen,
depending on your eyes. In another time,
in a deserted field, I lay naked as a lover
wrapped me in oil. I must have even walked
through high grass, and, knowing me, worried
about where bugs could enter.
Insects never crawl up the legs
in the paintings of the three Graces.
In those landscapes of the masculine

dream, men want to paint us, perfect,
from a distance, then break petals,
like a cloud or a swan.

Rapture Three

I

I never did anything dangerous as a child, except to fall
down the stairs, arms back, trying to fly. I never jumped
off roofs or dangled from rafters in an unfinished garage.
I was the girl who read library books on the playground
by the diamond linked fence, who only got asked
to jump rope when the other girls wanted someone
to turn the yellow plastic handle . . . When the phone rings
on this Friday night, it's a drunk friend of my husband's.
I answer, pretending I'm asleep because I'd rather not talk
to lonely alcoholics who call every weekend. Half my relatives
died from riding their snowmobiles too many times
to the bars all winter in the Upper Peninsula,
and my Italian mother reminds me that alcoholism is genetic
on my father's side. I'm lonely too, and wanted that voice
on the phone to be my husband's, in Detroit, on a crew
building an International House of Pancakes. It is just after
the third time they've found cancer, and I'm unwilling to leap
right back into the fight. I will have to soon enough: shots,
radiation, chemo; exercise, vitamins, visualization—
there's no point rushing the inevitable. The news is new,
and I deserve a chance to enjoy my hair awhile.
The local doctor whom I just ditched, first told me
of only two tumors, though he knew of four, and before
my biopsy, I told my friend, *Don't worry, I'm ninety-nine
percent perfect,* but there's more colonies of those bad cells
than even the doctor realized, and each one
might as well be a stop sign inside my heart, my abdomen,
my ovaries; scarlet sickle Cs cutting off my decades as
the CAT scanner looks for more with its radiating eyes.

II

As a child, I read through Andrew Lang's entire series
of folk tales, hue by hue: the *Violet Fairy Book,* the *Grey,*
the *Crimson.* And though I don't remember the stories—
except the one about the talking horse head on the barn wall
who advised the local shepherd girl—I still remember
where the volumes were shelved, to the right of the window
by the church where I attended Girl Scouts. Fairy tales all
have the same plot anyway, a boy-girl fighting a witch-ogre-troll,
and we either survive or are eaten. Today I told a woman
who didn't ask, I have no intention of dying soon.
The woman in expensive silver jewelry was just saying sorry
to hear I needed chemo again, having just watched
her mother go through it. What can they do to me that they haven't
already? The chemo and shots and bone marrow transplant?
I think maybe this time I won't beat it back.
But I can't think that. Tonight I met a children's writer,
who read aloud her latest picture book. I thought
of my own manuscripts; and of my own children
who likely won't exist. My picture books remain safe
at home in a box, but I morbidly think of my other
library treasures, and doubt anyone else will love them:
Memoirs of a Tattooist; Legends of the Bells: and 1930s
facsimile editions of *Babar.* I want to sleep, but I'm waiting
for my call, and can't stop thinking about my visit
to the oncologist today, the doctor who suggested I just let
the cancer spread since my marrow transplant had failed.

III

I pick up from the nurse my files and biopsy slides,
and in the next room, the chemo room, there's a man
in an easy chair, his legs are up, as if he's watching a Michigan
football game, and he's smiling. He looks a lot like my doctor,
and I have to glance again to see the I.V. bag dripping
into him. And maybe my mind put the doctor in that chair,
so the infusion would make him understand more
about being diseased than he does. What do you do
about something unwanted, like a tumor or a phone call
that keeps repeating? I consider having a portrait taken

of me while I still have hair, or buying six African hats.
I think of triple-piercing my ears, and purchasing polish
to paint my nails in green and magenta. But my adventures
should be bigger than what I can accomplish in three hours
at a mall. I should think constellations and transcendence
and becoming sunlight. My mother, a child of the fifties,
always wears red lipstick. There's something exotic about that,
something that would require a bit of courage. My husband
called at midnight, while I was undressing. I almost said,
teasingly, *I'm half naked right now,* when his drunken brother,
uninvited, picked up the line and started to listen.
I felt violated and angry, even though
I hadn't said anything a brother couldn't hear. I thought again,
I hate drunks: people who've chosen to be sick
and tell crude jokes at family dinners, turning into monsters
who come at you with knives, or fall asleep in cars
with the motors running. My stomach filled with acid, and I
wanted to hang up on my husband to make that second voice
go away. When the nurse is about to hook me up
for chemotherapy, it feels like that. Fear that something
dehumanizing or invasive or deadly is about to happen.
Then the chemicals enter, and the anti-nauseas dope me up,
and it's another day, and life's not bad if I'm in survival mode.

IV

I panicked, started to shake, right before my last biopsy,
done on a CAT scan table. The doctor ran me through
the machine then drew a line with black marker above
my tumor for the needle. So much depended on the tests
being benign, and I didn't want to go back to that unslept in
hospital bed, my bags not yet unpacked, for another five years.
That terror is what I feel now, but I'm in my own sheets,
alone, having received the voices of two drunk men
and my husband tonight. Now the telephone ringer is off
and I'm in double-layered sweats because this house is cold.
The window behind me is cracked, and sometimes I can smell
the neighbor's cigarette when he smokes outside
before leaving for his third shift job. I've seen them huddled
at the back entrance of the hospital, the skinny men

and women with their rolling I.V.s, smoking outside
in their bedclothes, despite everything. And I know cigarettes
might have brought them there, but I admire the tenacity
of those patients, to go out in their robes, blowing out
white smoke and breath, when most in that place
don't even leave their beds. And whatever I said earlier
about drunks, there's something sad about a life
without vices, which is why I won't quit coffee. Today
in the oncology office I saw that man grinning in an easy chair,
being dripped into, and I no longer felt separate as I have
for three years. Tonight I sit in the recliner with him
as the ceiling drizzles down a chemical rain and the man's
smiling head nuzzles my ear like the slurry voices
of alcoholics I've hung up on.

V

I can't sleep, and go into the barn to ask advice
of the talking horse. Will he prescribe the ten dollar cures?
Burdock root? Red clover? Green tea? Can he get me,
on the black market, that new lymphoma drug
concocted from Mammoth Cave fungus and the antibodies
of a mouse? I should have worn a costume
because I'm not the shepherd girl, and the horse
won't talk to me. He blinks, but then stares
with the same sandy eyes as a mounted buck in a tavern.
I remember, when young, I was convinced I would fly,
if only I could master the technique. I gathered
the house's bed pillows, spread them through the living room,
got a running start then leapt, and leapt. I practiced for hours,
not losing hope, while my mother with her red lips
never said a word: the carpet soft, the furniture cleared,
and nothing valuable in that room but me. It's odd,
when you're in peril, the adrenaline quickens. And before
the terror, like the pilot in the cockpit of an open biplane,
there's the joy of wind and danger and not being dead
that people pay to die for on Mount Everest. All week,
friends have been sending me presents, as if it were
my birthday. Cancer's like that, if you can survive:
a perilous birthday party on a rope bridge.

William Olsen

William Olsen's two books of poetry are *The Hand of God and a Few Bright Flowers* (University of Illinois Press, 1988), a National Poetry Series selection and a winner of the Texas Institute of Letters and Arts Award, and *Vision of a Storm Cloud* (Triquarterly Books: Northwestern University Press, 1996). Triquarterly will bring out a third book, *Trouble Lights,* in 2001. His poems have won him NEA and Breadloaf Fellowships, the Crazyhorse Poetry Award, a Poetry Northwest Helen Bullis Prize, a Pushcart Prize, and the Nation/Discovery Award. He teaches creative writing at Western Michigan University and at the MFA Program in Writing at Vermont College.

Paradise, Michigan

True, astronauts can see the wakes ships leave
and just as true the birds can see the stars
and it is also true that stars and fireflies
are equiponderant to human sight;
both sink into our very torment, our very
love of the turmoil we are to each other,
but only stars sink upwards from Superior.
The stars are nothing to the fireflies.
Both are prehistoric, both require night
to turn them on, both appear and reappear,
both hold one sky in common as do the
living and the dead, both strafe this dark thing
that sleeps in us all day until the sun falls
and the towns that we sleep in seethe anew
—as when all the lights in the house are burning.
You let your fingers brush my face the way moths
bang the screen door of this bright motel room
all they want. They're all the same, all
white as the moon and all wings till the last
little finger of your touch is everywhere,
and we awake to look across a graveyard
which is no graveyard at all, but Whitefish Bay.
Below a corrugated iron pier twelve miles
from Paradise,
300 plus corpses are out there under water;
all these ships went down too perfectly
and yet this planet's crowded as it is,
and we don't have a clue as to how to make
the world dance to our love, so we dream
far into another summer of consent.
We heard two hundred dollars puts your name
upon a star, we actually talk about it.
Need says whatever comes into our heads,
need invents a telephone book of stars,
holocausts a dial tone away.
We need motels, the numbered doors of sleep,

we need the slow cat of the water's lap and leer
to slush against no piers money can buy
a name for, we need money more and more,
we need our need to pay outside so far
it blinds us with the light of where we are.
Need is what we believe, and we believe it all,
we believe the bottom right hand of the moon
to be precise and ruthless to the very edge
of where precision ends, and where consent begins—
cars topping the sludge of Michigan's great dunes,
the glowworms of illuminated beech trunks,
and in the motel sleeping couples who
consent to private dreams, whereas the
waking consent to one world in common.
No two can see the same star even once
and so we dream of squandering two hundred dollars
to name one star, one strife so far away
distance seems a blinking toy.
This firefly upon your shirt is worth
a hundred billion stars named after us.
This firefly above the planet Mars
despises dying way up here or way down
there all the same, and if we stare at stars
to keep them distant or to bring them near
is all the same, and it is all the same
to sit out on a beach as it would be
to turn back to our motel room, its
tiny soaps and cheerfully logoed matchbooks.
If day and night are one, if Heraclitus,
guardian of the living and the dead,
has gone the way of light-years into night
and if it's death for soul to become water
and life for water to ascend to fire,
then if it's all the same I think I'll stare
a little longer as the good philosophers
weeping or laughing must have stared because
weeping or laughing all the same is fire,
the dead lucidity and the living ignorance,

the stars gone under without sinking us,
the love-drained bioluminescing fireflies
gone asleep in the grass . . . The dunes step off
soundless behind us and eat the stars.
Brave little lights are snuffed out everywhere.

In the Time of Blithe Astonishments

An Eastern rattler stopped its swallowing—
my tin-cut shadow abiding over its
pleasantly shiny scales so close no evening vapor

could come between them. In the pink shed of an open mouth
a field mouse with its two showing paws
curled up to the spiraled end of the fiddle ferns
in their orchestral settlements—
its rib cage a miniature bellows at work,

the wind that ate the prophets
stumbling through the trees draped with the huge
snowflakes of spiderwebs—

my teeth couldn't look away. Frogs stranded in their ring of scum,
all but their eyes hiding,
letting in strawpiles of threshing floor light,

Dante's flatterers up to their teeth in shit.
I had been taking in a blue-flag, the jawbone

of a cherub—

the horizon sinking upwards had clouds
thrown like spittle against it.
Something or
everything had doused the moon with gasoline
and set a match to it. For the smile of the highway.
The trucks have become bottomfeeders these evenings,

snapping up the mayflies in their headlights.
I couldn't look away until
the mouse actually gripped
the teeth of its punisher

for its foothold in this vast instant.

The Fold-Out Atlas of the Human Body
A Three-Dimensional Book for Readers of All Ages

The vertebrae are a ladder of moonlight
up and out of the perpetual nocturne
      of the body.

I open myself with the casualness
of a man having a smoke on a hotel roof.

The legs flip down
like ironing boards, and when I turn the page

each bone is numbered and charted and named in a
      dead language.
When the skeleton folds back, there are my organs—

my lungs, two punctured footballs, my tire-tread
      tendons;
fold out the lungs and a jungle of bronchiols

must be machete-d through
to reach the vertebrae espaliered by arteries.

Here and there a floral wreath of hissing nerves.
When the last tears are secreted,

and the eyes must be avulsed from the skull,
whoever will speak in praise of the passing face?

Whoever guessed the prayerbook
        was flesh?
The tongue turned all night like a sleeper in his bed,

having been possessed.
And there below the endlessly crouched ilium

is the place where the groin is missing out of tact.
The beginning embarrasses us all:

the red lights of my musculature
        are bad enough.
Blood washes its hands of blood,

there's nothing behind it,

and as for the heart,
there is s little door you can open

and reach inside:
bison drawings, cavemen, mothers, mud.

It has dreamed these things I never believed it would.

Anne-Marie Oomen

Ann (Anne-Marie) Oomen is a writer/storyteller/teacher whose work has been published in local, state, and regional magazines. She has written several plays, and her essays and poetry have won or placed in a variety of national contests. She currently teaches at Northwestern Michigan College and serves as chair of the Creative Writing Department at Interlochen Arts Academy. She lives in Empire, Michigan, with her husband, David Early.

What I Learned at "Down the Road" Café

Florence—I swap romance novels with her—
flips open the stainless coffee pot,
cigarette voice blaring
through a churn of shrill orders,

> *Leaving money—you know,*
> *bucks stashed away. Enough,*
> *I said, enough to get you out*
> *the door and down the road*
> *if things get rough.*

I brush and butter white toast.
Eggs pop through the window
like new men in our lives. Pans
crash in the Hobart

> *If things get rough? But you love Mac.*

The yolk's broke on my number ten, tearing
the melmac rim with gold.

> *Need another sunny side,* I say.

> *Always need another sunny side,* she says wicked like.

Florence drops extra ketchup samples
on her best trucker's hash browns.

> *See, you can't trust anybody*
> *forever. Sooner or later,*
> *we all float down the river,*
> *no one knows how or why,*
> *like in Last Escape—I said Last*
> *not Lust,—don't you confuse 'em—*
> *there's a kind of madness in us all.*

The lid snaps down, and splats a spray
of coffee on her scarlet nails.

> *Leaving money.*

Tucked in the trashy novels
stacked in my leaky closet,
I pretend it's not there,
never count the bills
that mark each sex scene,
but that old sweet witch, Flo,
she guesses, sees the pages in my eyes,
how the leaves turn yellow as old skin,
how corners tear up
and one escape leads to another.
Spring comes,
the river turns green and dark
as money,
just enough to get away
if you get to the last page of an old story
and you don't like the end.

Hiding Places for the Trout

I was still young the day I asked some men—
they were prisoners from the county jail
working the hill-country streams near the farm—
Making hiding places for the trout,
one answered, wiping his hands slowly on grass.

Hiding places—those deeper, cooler rushes in the shallows
just after a pile of rocks, or where tree trunks fall
after a lightning storm, the flood eating under roots.
Call them stresses, they make the water swirl
into something like scar tissue.

He said softly, *Where the creek flows faster
it makes a deeper hole, and way under,
it's quiet. Trout will go down, bed, and spawn.*
He asked for water, his voice like small rocks.
His hands were icy when I passed the glass.

All day the men worked against the current,
cutting dead trees, shoving rocks the size of radios
into the eddies. Nobody back then was planting the rivers,
you had to attract the fish and it was hard,
a county project—DDT had taken its toll

and not even a man in prison—he said
he had beaten his wife *to death*—
could resist this pleasure, this *encouragement*
was the word he used,
body aching like river and fish.

Oh child, you know water always follows the lowlands,
running into the deepest place, always
sliding into the cool under the wild—
yearning, driven, spawning out a life
on a hard gravel bed.

Because This Did Not Happen to Me

My farmer friend, driving the black Ford loaded with grain
into town, saw ahead the quick swerve, squeal and sudden jerk, heard
   the short deadly
crunch and knew for a thing so fast, so hard
not much could be said. He pulled over anyway, blinkers flashing
on the frosted grass, ran to it, and through the shattered window
he could reach her hands and touch her face and so he did.
They never spoke he said, but talked with eyes over the sirens
and with small, almost imperceptible squeezes of the hands.

And when I asked him what it was like, it took him weeks to tell
until finally, late over cheap wine his face changed
as if he'd found some small thing he'd looked for—there it was—
he said with calm, "Death came like a small seed . . ."
opened his thumb and forefinger slowly, and I took it
to mean when the husk opens in earth, but having never seen
how seeds or lives come apart, I was still afraid.

Awakening

I was raised on gravy, farm-cured hams,
creamed vegetables, all flavored with fat,

pies baked in lard crust, ripe fruit
ladled into great pots, sugared again, boiled down.

In the fall a man came to the screen door, his palm
turned up, suppliant. My mother fed him

so much he was sick. My brothers
argued about whether he was a bum or a hobo

before strolling back to fields to dig
carrots, turnips, potatoes, late tubers.

I watched him wipe spittle from his chin,
eat again, then lick his hands like a priest.

I raised my own palms and kissed,
tasted the roll of salt on my tongue,

tasted how bread and muscle connect,
how skin thins from too much licking,

how the palm could cave in
like a heart-shaped bowl

with a slim white spoon of
hunger running through.

Photo by Lois Palen

John Palen

John Palen (b. 1942) lives in Midland. His first book of poems, *To Coax a Fire,* was published by Green River Press in 1984. It was followed by *Liking the New Place Better,* privately printed in 1993, and *Staying Intact,* brought out in 1997 by Mayapple Press. A former newspaper editor, he teaches journalism at Central Michigan University, and has been married to cellist Lois Palen for thirty-five years.

When You Finish Your First Real Poem

it's as if you'd died: breath taken in,
let out slowly, and a full stop. A room
so still, the light bulbs are audible
as they sing in their sockets, high and pure

as castrati. Later, women will redden
their lips; two trumpet players will
leave school early, one to sound taps,
one its echo. The crazy old man

who lives among the graves will roam
and yell up and down the right of way,
his arms full of stolen bread. And all
because of you. And you've gone away.

Sirens

I'm upstairs at my desk, the winter
darkness pressing in on the window pane,
and you're downstairs playing the cello,
and we hear the siren start at the hospital,
an ambulance on a run. I know you hear it
as it maps the dark city; we can tell
when it reaches certain intersections
by the crazed blip, blip that replaces
the rising and falling wail. We can tell
where in the city it goes, almost name
the dark streets. How long has it been
since we ignored sirens, trusted they cried
for someone else and not for one of ours?

Slice of Life

His first wife never wanted to do it, his second never wanted
to do anything else, he tells us in the chummy intimacy
of men in a van, four strangers driving north in the rain
to open walleye season. "I like it," he says, "but my God,
when that's all you do, *all* you do . . ." He's not laughing,
this overweight laid-off autoworker with the sweet smile
and the freckles of a boy. He was in bed with his second
when he told her he was leaving. "You're gonna leave this?"
she taunted. "For what?" When he learned his first was cheating
he stayed up all night in their trailer, drinking beer,
a shotgun across his lap. If she had come home . . .

I don't know this man, who grips the wheel as if to drag
oncoming semi-trailers toward him through the rain—
headlights grainy in the mist, then chrome and red enamel,
the driver's male, shadowy bulk, the slam of the wake.
My driver shakes his head in disbelief, how close he was
to the edge that night. Even so, he says, he has brought
his piece, his .38. Jesus, what am I into, I wonder.
He slaps his waist, saying "Just in case," but there's no
gun there, nothing hanging over his belt but gut.

Pocket Watches

Soon no one will know
about the pendant pipe
or the pendant neck.
They won't be workaday
words much longer,
dome snap and back snap,
the push-piece tube,
the bezel and the olivette.

It's not only species
whose loss impoverishes.
When the century turns,
who'll distinguish between
Biseau and Bassine,
swing ring and hunter?
Who'll care if the knuckle
and the charniere are snug?

Sing a song for the pillar plate,
the yoke, the jewel screw.
Sing one for the balance cock,
and for me and you.

Two For Tin Pan Alley

1

It's spring, they say,
though a cold rain
spatters the pane.
It's spring, they say,
and they should know.

You haven't felt
the urge to call
or write at all.
It's spring, they tell me,
so let go.

I'll take the dog
around the block,
and skip a rock
through the fog;
I'll hum a blue
riff or two.
I'll do a monologue.

Then I'll put you
up on a shelf,
be my old self.
It's spring, they say,
so let go.

2

I've never cared for gourmet food,
don't look to see where the beer was brewed,
or notice the waiter's attitude.
I like the simple life with you.

I don't spend much on stylish clothes,
would rather smell lilacs than a rose.
Some trade in stocks; I'm not one of those.
I like the simple life with you.

Sunlight on a wooden floor;
morning paper, toast and tea.
Books at night, put out the light.
That's happiness for me.

Don't need to hunt endangered lions,
investigate the ancient Mayans,
discover a cure for dandelions,
just like the simple life with you.

Miriam Pederson

Miriam Pederson lives in Grand Rapids, Michigan, where she is an associate professor of English at Aquinas College. Her poetry has been published in several anthologies, journals, and small press magazines, including *The Third Coast: Contemporary Michigan Poetry* (1988), the *MacGuffin, Passages North, The Book of Birth Poetry, Sing Heavenly Muse, Kalliope,* and *Poets On.* Her poems in collaboration with sculpture created by her husband, Ron, are regularly exhibited in area and regional galleries.

Release

Not in the drumming of rain
or the animal purr, the rustle of leaves.
Not in the crackle of fire,
in the jangle of bells, the lap of the waves.
Not in the skip of stone across water,
the flapping of wings
or the cricket's sweet saw.
But in the heavy human sigh,
a-rhythmic as dust—
surrender of breath to the open air—
the blessed letting go.

Pears

Look how their ripening bodies
lean and shine
in the voluptuous October light.
The bowl cannot contain their curves—
they are threatening to expose everything.

When the painter mixes colors:
ochers, sunset reds, fertile greens,
the pears grow sincere and still,
winsome as homecoming queens,
ready to be fixed in the world
as they ought to be seen.

Trek

Land breathes water
in the jigsaw puzzle of dream.
The inhale and exhale
pieces itself into a hiking trek—
air so pure that muscles
feel no ache, the body feels no hunger.
It is enough to breathe and touch
the solid bones of earth
where drift and flow of rain and tide
fill furrow, crack and gully;
limestone, brimstone, feldspar, gypsum
each cupping its allotment.
Springs surface in unexpected gush,
sounding the vast exchange
where tread marks of hiking boots,
like perfect trilobites,
mark your passage
on this shifting landscape
somewhere between the Isle of Skye
and your own back yard.

Hard Work

What your grandfather did
with his hands should interest you
as you look at your own,
dexterous beyond his imagination.
Fingers calloused and stiff,
he pulled stones from his land
and stacked them like old grievances
to mark his boundaries.
He grappled with the earth
until his hand curled,
the handle of shovel or rake
defining his final infirmity.

Your occupation, you say,
demands nothing of this sort—
the switch and the keyboard,
the hobby and sport—
but look at your knuckles,
your capable palms—
what can they do
to make something last?

November

The brittle and the supple,
the bowed and the swaying,
the blushing and the fading,
the ripe and the hollow,
the broken and the whole,
the shimmering and the bruised,
the bent and the standing,
the hovering and the resting,
the golden and the copper,
the covered and the naked,
the soft and the hardened,
the sweet and the bitter,
the sterile and the fertile,
the chosen and the discarded,
the feathered and the smooth,
the rotted and the sprouting,
the rooted and the scattered,
the fallen and the risen,
the invisible and the impossible.

What Is Our Deepest Desire?

To be held this way in our mother's arms,
to be nestled deep in the warmth
of her body, her gaze,
to be adored, to overwhelm her
with our sweetness.
This is what we seek in chocolate,
in the food and drink and drugs
that stun the senses, that fill the veins
with the rich cream of well being.
What we take for lust—can it be, perhaps,
a heavy pang of longing to be swaddled,
close, close to the heartbeat of our mother?
No bucket seats, Jacuzzi, or even a lover's embrace
can duplicate this luxuriance,
this centered place on the roiling planet.

When the old woman, now small and light,
can be carried in the arms of her son,
he, at first, holds her tentatively,
a foreign doll,
but gradually, as the pool loses its ripples,
he sees his face in hers
and draws her to him,
rocking to the rhythm of her breathing.
This is the way to enter and leave the world.

Photo by Christine Garceau

Rosalie Sanara Petrouske

Rosalie Sanara Petrouske has had poetry and nonfiction published in the *Southern Poetry Review*, the *Seattle Review*, *Poets On*, *Passages North*, *Parting Gifts*, the *MacGuffin*, *The Grolier Poetry Prize Anthology*, *American Nature Writing*, and *The PrePress Awards Volume Two: Michigan Voices*, among others. A chapbook, *The Geisha Box*, was published by March Street Press in 1996. She is a graduate of Northern Michigan University with an MA in English. After having served two years as an AmeriCorps volunteer, she now lives with her husband, Bill Heuer, and her daughter, Senara, in Lansing, Michigan.

Moon through an Amber Glass

"Love took up the glass of Time,
and turned it in his glowing hands."

Alfred, Lord Tennyson, *Locksley Hall*

My father studied the moon through an amber glass.
He knew the sailor's warning about red skies,
the North Star as compass—I know some of my father.

He was gray-haired, over fifty at my birth.
I am told he rocked me, slapped my back at croup,
floorboards creaking and perhaps I recall the songs—
but I'm not sure. It feels like I've known only women
all my life, those figures that hover in aprons
and good advice, warmed by fresh-baked bread, white
potatoes, gravy drippings, and smelling of sun-dried sheets.

When I was three my father pulled me away from
the drunken neighbor who tried to take me to his house,
struck that younger man's face until it bounced
like a bloodied ball. This scene is clear to me.
I feared my father then, but afterwards with fists
still bleeding, he rocked me until my trembling stopped.

The women in my family raised their voices.
It took my father longer to anger—to meet that shrillness
with his rage. He was an old man who talked about
the geography of the earth, the molten layers
and sedimentary rocks moved by wind and rain.
When I ran high fevers, he walked to St. Francis,
asked the nuns for pills to break fevers, to save
the life of his little girl.

He carved a wooden cross for my older sister,
Rose-Marie, who was born a "blue baby."
He named me after his favorite niece,
the girl that worked at a five and dime,
died from a brain tumor at seventeen.

I grew up believing I would never reach
my eighteenth birthday.

In my only picture of my father as a young man,
he wears a gray suit, his shirt collar starched
high and white, his gray felt Homburg at an angle
to his broad forehead.

In that photograph, I do not recognize the man
I knew at Stonington who covered a wasp sting
    in my palm with his mouth,
        and pulled the poison into him.

A Postcard from My Mother

I flip pages in the book I'm reading and a postcard
falls into my lap: Birch Lodge on Trout Lake, Michigan.
A two-story building with an upper balcony leans
into tones of sepia. Ghostly trunks of birch frame
a gabled roof. A man in baggy trousers and a panama straw
feeds a fawn. On the back of the card, my mother has written:

June 1935

Dear Folks:
    This is the fawn and Mr. Moore again.
I am sending a few recipes; one is
apple cup. It sure is swell.

At seventeen, my mother was a maid at the Lodge
where newlyweds left her a fifty-dollar tip and a bottle
of champagne for keeping their shoes straight in the closet.
My tiny-waisted mother hung starched sheets on lines
in the Lodge's backyard, thinking of the red dancing dress
she would buy with her summer's earnings.

Later, her first husband pushed her from his Buick
onto the Dollarville Road after the Fourth of July dance,
drove away and never looked back to see her tumble
into the water at the bottom of the ditch. She lay, feeling
her stomach tremble with my sister's kicking
under the front of her torn skirt.

And I think about this baby moving softly inside me,
a girl child already loved by her father.
I wonder if some other autumn my daughter
will find a note in my handwriting, take it
to the window to see its message more clearly.
Outside the sky darkens. I put the postcard away.
In this quiet room, I feel three women pause
in the simple light of early November.

Angels

I drive through the darkened streets
of Christmas Eve, past St. Paul's
and midnight worshippers sheltered
behind oak doors. Along Arch Street,
neighbors have lighted votive candles
inside paper sacks, fireflies flickering
in the snow.

The baby kicks above my ribs,
her foot pushing hard.
Her skin must be gossamer as angel wings—
light shining through them, her hair
fine as the spun glass enfolding
Christmas trees of my childhood.

A bitter cold night; Mother wraps gifts,
curling ribbon through her fingertips
while the old Victrola plays music from the '20s.
Grandmother hangs glass stars,
bells and amber balls that reflect my round face.
Where have those stars fallen?
It is only memory that keeps them alive—trembling.

Grandmother calls me little fraulein,
teaches me the mysteries of the rosary.
In her seventy-fourth year, she names stars
and leaves as we gather spring pussywillows
at Mill Pond—ironwood, blue beech, basswood,
bur oak, and there, in the fall, above the black willow,
she points to the north star, first star of the night,
the beginnings of the dippers, the taut bow of Orion.

Mother pulls me into her aproned warmth,
shows me how she flutes an apple pie.
Now, in her sixty-ninth year, I comb her thinning hair
watch her walk with palsied steps, the bones in her hands
quiver like an aspen buffeted by winter winds.

In my dreams those women scrub and mend, hum
their working tunes, pray and mourn, celebrate
their fears: My mother, of being young, abandoned;
my grandmother, of growing old, alone.
Tonight, I drive to the chorus of their voices,
their heartsong moving, the flapping of a thousand
wings inside me.

The lights of home shine down from Harkin's Hill.
It is late and time to go to sleep. My little *fraulein*
hears my voice and the beating of my heart.
She curls a foot against the hollow in my stomach.
I imagine a hand tucked beneath her chin
as she grows still in her dark murmuring.

Susan Blackwell Ramsey

Susan Blackwell Ramsey was born in Detroit in 1950. She earned her BA from Kalamazoo College and liked the town so well that she still lives there with her husband and three children. Her work has appeared in publications from the *Atlanta Review, Poetry Northwest,* and *Primavera* to *Studio Potter,* as well as in the Storyline Press anthology, *The Muse Strikes Back.*

Aftereffects of Bell's Palsy

Having a good and bad ear comes in handy.
My bad ear, victim of a surgeon's saw
screaming through bone to free a facial nerve,
has lost the very highest range of sounds—
bats, telephones or sirens at a distance,
mosquitoes if they're male, small children whining,
regret, ambition's wheedlings, most tactful hints.
Banshees can keen on my ridgepole all night long,
and, exhausted, watch me leave for work,
brisk and refreshed from sleeping good ear down.

My undiminished left ear can perceive
the beginnings of nightmare in a sleeping child
two rooms away behind a closed door, hear
the click of covert glances at a party,
the first drop on the roof of the first rain
of April, surmise the maiden name and color
of the eyes of the grandmother of the boy
my daughter sits thinking of, based on her breathing.
It can hear loneliness seven lamp posts down
the street, slamming like a screen door in the wind.

Metonomy

She's forbidden her dog to die
if she's not home. "No coming home
to find a dead dog. Got it?" She plans
to have him cremated,
to mix his ashes with clay
and shape him
into something permanent.

She has offered to do the same thing for her mother.
Her sister shudders, declines half. Her mother
likes the notion of being
both urn and ashes,
container and contained.

She sees her daughter at the potter's wheel,
hands slippery with love
bowls spiraling out around her,
mute mouths open
like storytellers.

Such a cliche to be spread on wind or water,
drafty, vagabond.
She trusts her daughter
to defend her with craft,
shaping a future where whatever remains
nestles again in its own brittle clay.

Our Third Wedding Reception This Year Hits Its Stride

The floor's packed, partners optional. They play
"Down on the Corner," segue into "Shout";
we jump and hunker, silk dignity out—
grown and molted. Now it's "YMCA."
This homosexual anthem has become,
in the heavy hand of some god of irony,
the current wedding classic. The elderly,
the shy—this dance accommodates everyone,
like a favorite uncle, somehow still unmarried,
who flirts with great aunts, spins the flower girl,
waltzes gently with his fragile mother,
finds car keys, coaxes laughter from the harried
hostess, so the rest of us can clap and twirl
and briefly notice that we love each other.

Tripping

FOR VICKI

Sugar, we're leaving tonight.
Don't worry about the kids—his guilt will nest them
cozy as goslings until you come home sound.
You can bring them shiny stones and souvenir spoons
and beer cans from Enid, Oklahoma.
But tonight we're gone,
windows all the way down cause we don't care
what happens to our hair, the night trees passing,
their hands clasped over our heads,
music on the radio so sad that the headlights swim and blur
and then so hot we shimmy in our seats,
have to stop the car,
get out and stomp until the music ends
too soon.
We'll scorn the interstates, stick to the back roads.
Not outlaws, though—that wakes their posse instinct,
and besides
the hours are long and you have to be willing to travel.
We'll be the underground, we'll infiltrate,
slipping into town with the groundwater.
They'll think we've always been there, past the edge
of town, out by the water, where the porch
has two rockers,
one with, one without arms.
The pillowcases smell of wind and grass, the water's well.
There is no time there—we'll return the night
before we left, no matter how long we stay.
Your job will be
to name that big dog nudging at your hand,
prop your heels on the porch rail, and watch
the fine pearl silt of happiness float down
into the crater blasted in your heart.
When it is full, we'll go.

The Sword

Power is a sword in a ditch by the side of the road,
half buried in mud and dung, its ornate hilt
gleaming through last year's grasses and burdock leaves.

Say that a woman, on her way back from market, maybe,
load-light with coins in her pocket and headed for home
sees the gold glint and tugs till the whole length is loosened.
What then?

She'll make an odd sight dragging that thing beside her,
trying not to get muck on her market clothes. Many a man
would believe he was doing right to wrestle it from her—
no business with such a thing, she could injure herself—
and stride off whistling while she rubbed her wrist.

But say that the day is late, the road deserted,
the lights from the windows beginning to glow in the yards
as she walks the last mile, switching her grip on the hilt
so the shaft runs down through her fist, a good walking stick,
its tip toothing into the roadway and pulling her on.

Think of the uses she'd find for it, getting it home,
such flexible metal, strong and sharp. It could be
lever and lightning rod, cleaver and chimney probe,
source of straight furrows for seeds in a cottage garden
and brace to keep doors shut against the night.

But hearing the echo in the back of her brain from her brothers
"Women—they ruin good tools by perverting their use..."
being no fool, recognizing
the true nature of this sword, she keeps it hidden
so no one will be tempted to take it, learning
to get the good of it without cutting herself.

Greg Rappleye

Greg Rappleye was born in Grand Rapids in 1953 and grew up in Jackson and Indian River. His poems have appeared in a variety of literary journals, including *Quarterly West*, the *Southern Review, Sycamore Review*, the *Santa Barbara Review, Prairie Schooner*, and *Passages North*, and in *The PrePress Awards, 1992–1993: A Sampler of Emerging Michigan Writers*. His first full-length collection, *Holding Down the Earth*, was published in 1995. He currently lives near Grand Haven with the painter Marcia Kennedy.

Charon in August

FOR JACK RIDL

The languid afternoon. Insects,
droning on into the night. Charon lies
at the bottom of his rowboat,
thinking about his life.
No classes this summer. No deliveries
to the other side. That's fine with him.
And if he's no longer wraith-like,
he can handle that. He's grown a little bald,
a touch of gray in the beard now, yes,
but still cuts a romantic figure.
Past the golden light of dusk, into
the growing darkness, he listens to the river
push against the gunwales. How many poets,
he wonders, have I ferried across this river?
Vergil, Homer, Horace, Ovid, Lucan.
Dante himself, who passed out
after too many "drinkies" at the airport,
and had to be loaded by hand
into Charon's boat. Then the endless stream
of acolytes, showing up after the readings
for the parties at his house. Eating
Charon's nacho chips, drinking all his beer,
Cerberus, his three-headed dog,
yowling apoplectically in the yard.
And the local bards! My God,
their egos! He's tired of hearing
about so-and-so's grant application,
and the terrific contract that one got
with Graywolf of Knopf.
For a year now, his own book has gone
outward and back, outward and back.
He thinks about Jesus though and smiles
despite himself. There was a poet!
He showed up late, weird story about the trip,
stigmata leaking all over the boat.

Spent three days in bed
with *delirium tremens,* then flew off
to collect a genius grant.
"In the middle of my life,
in the middle of my life..."
Isn't that what Dante kept muttering,
nursing a glass of pinot noir,
after speaking to Charon's seminar
on disembodied poetics?
Charon mouths these same words,
touches his hand gently to his forehead,
snuggles back against the bottom of the boat.
Feeling kind of hungry, he thinks.
Wonder if Mrs. Charon wants to step out
for a bite. Maybe some ribs.
He knows this all night barbecue
near the bridge to Circle 6. He feels a twitch,
and shifts his weight against the keel.
What did his chiropractor say?
A swollen disk, amid
the lower lumbar vertebrae.
Not going to pole so hard
he decides, lays his head back
and closes his eyes. Just resting.
Perhaps the tiniest cat nap. Slowly,
his breathing slows. Above him the stars,
not yet fixed,
twist into funny animal shapes,
like a clown's balloons,
testing their myths across the sky.

Fidelity

I woke up when the rain began.
The hot August night and a storm
blowing in across the lake.
The lightning started,
and the wild hosannas of the trees.
I went to close the windows on the porch,
then opened the door to watch the rain,
ponding in the yard and the street beyond.
The lightning lit up and lit up the air,
brilliant and incendiary. Then
the shock of thunder, answering
and rolling away.
Had anyone been looking,
it might have startled them.
The body of a man, suddenly framed
in an open doorway.
But I wanted the mist
and the cooling breeze of the storm.
I walked back to the bedroom
and found you awake in the dark.
"Where did you go?" you asked,
fright and sleep searching for balance
in your voice.
And lightning lit up our room
where I stood leaning against
the frame of the door, while the rain
went on, falling and falling
in the dark of the yard.

Terrible

The man from room 8
is washing and waxing his car.
It's a black Ford, with flames
stenciled on the doors,
and the word "Terrible"
inscribed in an elegant cursive
on the pillars of the roof.
I think I know his life. I lived it
at Red's Motel, on a stinky bayou
near Hopedale, Louisiana.
We called it "Hopeless,"
as in, "Maybe I'll call you,
when I get back to Hopeless."
It was a bad place, full of oil workers
and helicopter pilots.
I was driving the coast
in a rental sedan, setting up deals
to cut and pack fish. I carried
a leather sample case,
a book of account,
and a 9 mm Glock
with two fully-loaded clips.
No one believes the part about the gun.
But there are things I learned
you wouldn't necessarily believe.
The truth is, I only fired it once.
I bought twelve honey rock melons
and a six-pack of beer
in Pascagoula, Mississippi.
"I'm having a picnic," I told the clerk,
and drove out to a swampy field
near the Pascagoula River.
A 9 mm Glock will flat play hell
on a honey rock melon.
Sometimes at night I'd lie in bed,
a thousand insects

tapping against the screens,
drinking whiskey and cleaning the gun.
I didn't mind Red's Motel,
and I didn't mind carrying the Glock,
and I want to tell you
that if a situation arose,
I would have used it.
What I can't say is what happened.
Let's suppose a moment of clarity
in a burning cane field
outside New Iberia,
where someone finally realized
the man he worked for
was a terrible man.
I tossed the Glock off the ferry
that crosses the Mississippi River
between Vacherie and Lutcher.
And now I'm six doors down
from room 8.
So I remember what it's like,
living in a bad place,
cleaning and polishing the one thing
you know will get you home.
The allegiance you build to it,
day after terrible day.

Photo © 1997 by Alan Zinn

Danny Rendleman

Danny Rendleman is the author of six books of poetry: the latest, *The Middle West*, published in 1995 by Ridgeway Press. His work has appeared in over 350 publications in the last thirty years, including the *American Poetry Review*, *Field*, *Rolling Stone*, and *Epoch*. He teaches writing and literature at the University of Michigan-Flint. He is the recipient of three Michigan Council for the Arts Creative Artists grants, the Richard Hugo Fellowship at the Centrum Arts Colony in Washington, and most recently the UM-Flint Faculty Achievement Award for Teaching Excellence.

Cheese Lines, Flint, Michigan

Gray lines of women at the North Flint Plaza—
Waiting their due, surplus cheese and butter
We can't use, the lines that shuffle
Down the weed-split sidewalks,
Past the boarded-up display windows
Of The Fair, United Shirt, Nobil Shoes,
While at the curb monstrous green Buicks
Idle and rust. The day is overcast,
Threatening drizzle, feinting autumn
And further calamity. I drive by, this,
My old neighborhood, this shopping center
Our hangout, a pack of Luckies secreted
Behind a loose brick, our leather jackets
With The Royals on the back,
Our pointed Flagg Bros. shoes, and duck ass hair.
We the pioneers. These the women we went
To school with who never moved away,
Whom we never spoke to, let alone dated,
Or whom we desired, but never let on.

Flint, a city as hard and abrupt as its
Quick-bitten name. Home of Chevy-in-the-Hole,
Where men like my father got used to days
Etched thin and gritty as Mohawk vodka
And steel shavings in their aching hands
And little wretched patches of back-yards
Where they maybe played catch
With their kids before the noon whistle.
See how easily those women are forgotten?
Even in poems devoted to their bad luck.

Neighborhood

Remember the boy in the corner house,
the slow boy, face like a moon in the attic window,
his mom old enough to be his grandmother,
she of the babushka and black Dr. Scholl's
and the garage with the wicker wheelchair?

—or was that next door, father Bob
with the hearing aid the size of a fist,
daughter Bobbie whose reputation
stretched over three counties, and mother
what's-her-name who went absolutely crazy
and moved to Saginaw?

Or was it Owosso—somewhere other,
some place where only Mexicans or coloreds
congregated. Like the Garcias,
who came from Keokuk, and once worked
at a factory that only made pig nose rings.

Or was that the Stewinskis, displaced people
from the Ukraine or Poland or Hungary
or the other side of the tracks, mild blond folk
who spoke quietly, whose words were a susurrus
of secrets and fear ten years after the war,
their house with the only piano on the block
and Easter eggs as elaborate as Tiffany's.

Their house smack dab across from the Lees,
and who in the hell were they—dreary little hovel
set back from the road—none of them seemed related,
or seemed too related: three men, two women, God knows
how many kids, all girls, arrayed in dirty flowered dresses,
but one boy, hulking and sullen and fearsome—
we all boasted scars of *his* ill will.
And then one day all gone, not a sign of them
but for a litter of mongrels on the porch,
mother and pups all dead.

The photos show a rutted road, an infinity of gray.
This is why we sometimes dream in black and white,
why some dreams refuse to dissipate but stay,
the scars of memory pricking our lives like a testament.
Were we to look out our windows, would we see
the slow boy emerging finally from his attic room,
finally bidding his mother good-by, off to downtown
to seek his way or come home bloodied once more?

Did Cathy and Bobbie's mother ever come home
from Saginaw, ready to try it all over again—
or stay there, get the doctor to fix her up for a new life,
peel the old skin off, provide a remedy, shine her
like an apple for the world to eat?

The Stewinskis, the Lees—are they out there
in that blurred landscape just beyond the glass,
in the photograph, still? Static, unmoved, unmoving,
or were they, *are* they like us—the house where I lived
in the neighborhood, one day abandoned, the next
torn down, the next appearing in dreams
we wake from raging and terrified.
Or do not wake from however hard we try.

Solving for Zero

It is 2:45 in Mrs. Toomey's
Math class on a Friday afternoon.
And it is June 6. The summer stretches
Out golden and cicada-ridden outside
The dark-brown casement windows,
Still garlanded with construction
Paper suns and tulips and beachballs,
And the summer writhes before us.

We are about to explode.

Next to me are Linda Harper's
Thighs, upon which my eyes do linger.
Once, much later, I was stunned into silence,
And I suppose a kind of worship,
When I came upon a stand of white pine
Near Charlevoix, an island of perfect calm
And glow. That's how I felt
About Linda Harper's thighs:
The slow, incredible sweetness of the arc
From hip to knee, the thin gabardine,
Taut and lucky. Behind me, Paul, oh, Johnson,
Is burping. He will grow up to die
Young and earnest in Viet Nam. To my left,
Stan Gold is picking his nose.
He will grow up and win entrée
To MIT and publish ground-breaking articles
And marry badly and take his life
With a razor in a bathtub. But,
Though I would kill to touch Linda Harper's thighs,
She thinks I'm a dink and she's right.
Even though I'll grow all the way up
And grow old and be happy,
I'm a cipher in her eyes—those hazel eyes
Already set on cheer-leading
And Homecoming and marrying a lawyer

Or two. And so she did.
What is the square root of 144? asks Mrs. Toomey.
Stanley raises his hand, Paul burps, I slump
Lower in my chair behind Tonya, the fast girl
Who lives down the lane. We all fidget
And sweat and suck in our breath
At the afternoon dying outside. Did I tell you
Mrs. Toomey had a wooden leg?

Did I tell you she loved us, adored us,
Would give up her life for our little seventh-grade hearts?
And of course we made fun of her and her leg,
Her sad print dress that stuck in her butt
When she rose to write on the board, solving for zero.

Right now, this moment, sitting in my backyard
Watching wrens clatter and mate, chitter and mate,
Fritter lives away mating and mating, right now
I can tell myself I am better off not ever having
Linda Harper's thighs. Trouble and heartbreak
And a world of woe, no doubt.

My summer stretches before me, right here,
Just beyond the hand I raise to the heavens.
It's still golden and cicada-ridden,
And I am silent and worshipful. And so it also
Remains, just outside the brown windows
Of Pierson School, waiting like a young girl's body,
Just beyond reach or wish.

It is 2:46 in Mrs. Toomey's math class, Friday, 1957.

Jack Ridl

Jack Ridl lives with his wife, Julie, and their clumber spaniels, Stafford and Bobbie Jean. He teaches at Hope College, where he started the Hope College Visiting Writers Series. Along with Peter Schakel, he is the author of *Approaching Poetry: Perspectives and Responses* (St. Martin's Press). In 1997, he was named Michigan Professor of the Year by the Carnegie Foundation.

I Am Wearing Your Shirt

FOR MY FATHER

When your words left
your hands, the only place
silence holds us to the earth
opened. Somewhere a child
opened a door. Somewhere
a mother looked out a window.

You lived in your hands—alive
in bread dough, along the handles
of tools, holding the endless
usefulness of rags. "In all
things, a firm grip," you told me,
and at the end, you wanted only
your hands.

The snow that comes in the mornings
brings each of your words. The water
forms around your and, your either, not
and yes. They land, they just land.
Sometimes they fall all day, and into
the next. Sometimes they melt before noon.

You never waited. In the Spring,
you forced the shoots, even
the blooms. The trays waited
on the coffee table, the refrigerator,
the floor of the family room. We gave
one to anyone who stopped. They
were gone by May.

Yesterday, I found a photograph. I'm
sitting on your shoulders. Or is it you
sitting on your father's shoulders? Or
is it your grandfather sitting
on his beer wagon, holding
his team of tired horses?

At the funeral, you walked through the house
collecting your garden tools, cookbooks, and
sweatshirts while each visitor laid the bud
of a rose on your chest. They formed a heart
within the heart of your arms and folded hands.
I imagine them opening in your ashes.

Every morning for fifty-one years, you
woke and began by whispering, "This
is the best part of the day," and laid
your arm across her back.

I am wearing your shirt. Now,
when I walk, I wear your hat. In
the garden, I wear your gloves.

Here the land is flat. You
lived in the clay hills,
always at an angle.

Growing up on Goat Shit Hill,
looking out over the sullen
open hearths, the tired smoke
of the mills, the smudged strip
of heartless coal, you took shot
after shot at the hoop your father
rammed into the ridge behind
your house, knowing any miss
could send you down a mile
after the disrespected ball.

The house is cold now, cold
as Spring turning itself
into bloom. We wait at the window.

Your God wanted no attention at all.

Yesterday, when I dug into our garden's
matted earth, I felt your hand slide
into mine as if it were putting on
a glove. We went together
into the awkward ground, turned the soil,
let it slip between our fingers.

You always stepped aside
to let every question have its way.

Where have you walked
in a year? The center
of snow . . . the center of
each amen . . . of every
word we've tried to keep.
Now, on this still April afternoon,
a year to the day you came
to stay within us, the trees'
negative space waits for leaves.

Wearing your shirt, I look out into
the wood, where the end of each branch
touches the air's one silence.

How you loved this dust, this
light on the side of the house.

First Cut

The night before,
eight of the players
slept. Each of the rest
lay wondering if his name
would not be on the list.
"Tomorrow we'll post
first cuts," Coach had said.
"If you're on the list,
you're still on the team.
If not," and he shrugged.
Twenty-two now went to look,
hoping to see themselves
among the chosen.
For years these names had been nothing
more than something they had answered to.
But today, hurled back
to the earth's first days,
they could feel the finger
of the first caller point
then choose. God said, "Smith,"
and Smith walked on among the elect.
On the wall, next
to Coach's office door,
the list. Some came
early, stood, stared,
and left. Some waited.
Coach had told them
not to say a word.
Some held out past lunch,
then gave in, went,
and saw. At practice,
Coach called together
the chosen. "All right,"
he said, "you've made it
this far. There will be one more
cut. Twelve of you will make it.

We'll go one more week. OK,
wind sprints." The others
looked for something
else to do, wished
they'd never tried, felt
a fire burning around their name.

Against Elegies

I'm tired of death's allure, of
how the old beggar makes me think
that rowing across the river is
somehow richer, more serious, than
the center of a pomegranate or my
dog's way of sleeping on his paws.
I'm tired of "the beauty of the elegy,"
of the tone deaf lyricism of it all. I
want death to listen for awhile
to Bud Powell or Art Blakey or
to have to stare for seven hours
at Matisse. I want him to do
stand-up and play the banjo, to
have to tap dance and juggle, to
play Trivial Pursuit and weed
my garden. I'm tired of how death
throws his voice, gets us
to judge a begonia, a song
in the shower, a voice, old dog.
I want life's ragged way
of getting along, the wasted
afternoon and empty morning, the
sloppy kiss. I want to stagger
along between innings. I want
the burnt toast, the forgotten note,
and the lost pillow case, the dime
novel and the silly putty of it all.

John Rybicki

John Rybicki was born and raised in Detroit. His most recent book is *Traveling at High Speeds* (New Issues Press). His work has appeared in *North American Review*, the *Quarterly*, and *Yankee*, among other publications. He is the recipient of grants from the American Academy and Institute for Arts and Letters, the Michigan Council for the Arts, and the Pen/American Center.

Julie Ann in the Bone Marrow Unit, Zion, Illinois

Ah Dame, I don't know how else to love you
sometimes so I just start juggling. I'm on the street

three floors below your hospital window,
lofting fish or birds that graze against my hands

and fly off; juggling cancer cells and carnations;
slipping in the bowling pin

we snuck out of that alley in Maine. Then I'm juggling
freight trains, and angels, and elephants,

dropping them all. I don't care. So long
as you can stand near your high window and laugh,

so long as you stand near your hospital bed
clapping your hands.

Becoming

I strip open
these walls, peeling
my way to stubbed
corn. Madness
to rise from that
hive, sleep,

its rainbows flying
out of my mouth
like ribbon.

I can't go on and there
is no pill in my bag for that.

Riches? Man, I have
washed in the steam
of a woman's breath,
gone off into the trees,
singing.

It is not enough
to cough up the day
like a hand grenade, make trash
can music, heave yourself out
through the percussionist's drum.
You have to live forever,
slap your paint against the day
as at a fence.

All I want is to love,
to scatter the wind
and call it back
to my hands. God above,
I can't go on,
and thank you for this day.

Begin

Pacing around my house and grabbing chip
and saying *chip,* floating it over light and under light
and sticking it into my other hand. Other hand doesn't eat it.
Try wall but wall doesn't open up and swallow chip.
I say wall and lay one flat hand against and I get swallowed in.
Holding onto chip, rough knifing it, trying to slice my way out.
Chips snaps in half. I say *dark* and name it *dark.*
I'm whispering to my wife who lives inside the movie screen
that's trying to kiss the movie screen I'm swallowed in
when there's no need for whispering. Something rings and I
name it *phone rings* but not out loud which would be a whole
phrase of me naming things. One of my students hears me
whispering so now I know my voice doesn't live in my elbow,
or leak through my knees, or peck its way out through my ribs
because I've tried all that. And either I'm silent and he's
hearing me think, or I'm whispering, so let's call it *whispering.*
"Were you sleeping," he asks? *No, just whispering.*
"I leave your class and your whispering
doesn't add up to anything for me," but he's not saying that.
"I'm naming things, too," he says but he's not whispering.
I'm inside the wall with the phone line leading inside
my movie screen naming things and shimmering.
My wife's movie screen is rubbing its belly against
my movie screen, and I'm listening to her naming things
and him naming things and no one at all is whispering.
"When I leave your house," student is saying in hard language,
    ball-peen, "I'm on fire." Now I'm checking my—
I'll call them—*arms* for fire, and pushing them through
the movie screen. "I leave your house and even God's lips
at the end of your street can't blow my fire out," student says
    while I'm whispering *earth* and *dirt* and *concrete,*
and things—they're appearing below his feet
so he's not falling while I'm whispering.

King

James' Husky King disappears under one tiny square of snow in the ghetto. We're in our t-shirts yelling "King! King!" off the porch come morning and there's nothing but white powder out there, white tundra, the heart's wildness. We're shouting "Here King!" from the porch where nights before we had cracked off rounds from James' revolvers, "You gotta let 'em know what you have or they'll come get some." On that porch in just our t-shirts yelling to the hound over such sweet desolation—electric lines, cinder block walls, monkey bars thick boned with snow. We don't see him. The white kettle of breath steaming up, the hound bounding suddenly out of white powder and pounding towards us with these iceburg hunks spilling off his coat. And sweet Christ if it wasn't wild enough, all those cinder block walls, I-beam and brick miles ignite, turn to white ash, like it's God's breath reforging an iron cake. The Belle Isle and Ambassador bridges pull down suddenly in a gust; the hound hauling himself out of deep powder in arch after sweet arch, every drop of light and heart and energy burning forward through his muscles, burning out through his eyes and trained on us. Every river of concrete, every fuming car, every power line is just bad music, a mistake he can fix by letting the snow settle over him, then thundering out of the earth come morning.

Interlochen Center for the Arts

I'm tired of being locked up, living inside a high C note, bedding down in a soprano voice that never draws breath. Tonight my legs took root in a liquid earth. I tried floating out to sea until I was dead: I wanted to know who I'd travel back to and love one last time before I drowned. Every morning pianos float past my cabin window like lazy barges; children dive in and find harps hidden in piles of thorns; and then these four kids line up beside four maples and started dragging their bows across each trunk as if sawing them down; as if each tree were a string on a giant cello they were born to play to perfection.

I walk around all day punching one pointed toe into the earth in front of me to make sure it's still there. I mean, it's like someone tore a piece of cloth off Christ's coat and we're all floating around on it. I'm up there, up here and by the third week I've stopped using like or as. I'm 90% sure I'm dead, and that's heaven tuning up out there.

There's a terror in this world. I'm afraid to see anyone I know: ma, pa, Joey, Leo.... I'm terrified I dreamed their voices, dreamed the people around me: highway tides of drivers sputtering to life when I approach; men and women with jackhammer drills, library cards, butcher knives; terrified I have arms and hands I can't see, arms and hands I slip into their bodies when they get close, and with one hand around the back of each heart like a baby's head, start pumping them to life, so I'll have someone in the world to talk to.

Photo by Jim Powell

Herbert Scott

Herbert Scott teaches at Western Michigan University, where he is the Gwen Frostic Professor of Creative Writing. He is also editor of the *New Issues Press* poetry series. His poems have appeared most recently in *Michigan Quarterly Review*, *Kenyon Review*, and *Poetry Northwest*. A letterpress edition of *The Wishing Heart* will appear from Sutton Hoo Press in 2000. He is the author of three previous collections of poetry.

The Blue Turtle

We cup our hands
against distance, build

a leanto of knuckles,
kindle a small flame

in the palm of space.
What we own, what we carry.

It is only in the blood-beating
tick of our hearts

against the almost human
whistle of winter

the small blue turtle
each day makes up

a new world, disordered
and reckless, of surprises.

Bees

The bees found an entrance below
the eavestrough, a passage
where the stucco gaped an invitation,
early last fall, too late,
I would think, to establish
winter store. Their business
kept me away from overflowing
leaves wedging drains,
so that autumn rains brewed
and rose and fell
into window wells two stories below.
And I with no courage or will
to force their fury
let them build and save
until winter closed the door,
then bought the poison to apply.
With ladder, spray, and caulk
I sealed them in their vault and thought:
this is the last of it. But in the nights
that followed, that turned to months,
in that dark house I listened
to their darkness, their blind assault
that seemed like sleet within the walls,
those starved, bony bees chalking
their maze, marking blind alleys
again and again, until I longed
for any way to wrench them loose,
set them free, stop their ticking.
When would they settle, give in,
begin to write their pleas for forgiveness,
their last wishes, their wills?
In what mute remonstrance
would they inhabit
that numb peace before drowning?

Mime

That feeling of someone there
so she turns to peer over her shoulder.
But the sidewalk clicks empty
and no one at the open window she passes.
Still, that unease, like the distress
of curtains settling, the failing lung of air
as she turns again, and, oh, there is
someone, someone familiar,
as if she has stepped aside
and sees herself as she might be.
It must be one of those
street mimes, one of those
who gather a living becoming
what one cannot become,
becoming her walk, her grace
and particularity, her flesh
as it furls and dips, playing
to those who watch just out of reach,
with a smirk, with shoulders winking,
arms straight at the sides
but the hands tipped outward,
spilling the cooled tea;
so that as she turns
there is only that figure turning
in pirouette, its skirt wheeling
in the brilliant silk of motion, the face
already lost in the unaccountable distance.

The Most Terrible and Beautiful Thing

The earth opening, bodies startled
from their graves, lungs like butterflies.
Hearts like matches striking

catch, take hold, not all
at once, but each in its own dark time.
"Is this the moment we were promised?'

They touch each other like the blind.
The past is future, the future closed
forever in the past. Each thing returns

to its beginning, crops to the fields, pasture
to woods, rivers clear to pure thin tongues.
Machines are put to sleep like toothless dogs.

The assassin sips his breakfast coffee
robbed of purpose. Rain climbs
the morning sky. At first, a blessing,

the dead in the arms of their loved ones.
And yet, these poor souls, how mystified
and fierce to see their lives erased,

to know the certain term of infancy,
the seed ungiven as fathers steal them
from their earthly home.

How bitter is that death called birth
as our brief time begins, is spent,
and God will not relent.

In a Field of Sunlight

We will walk into the field
of goldenrod splintered
by the sun's foolishness.
We have been there before,
after a rain,
when the water streamed
like the grain of wood
around obliterations
of limb, and knots
of mourners recalling
other losses, other rains.

The mind as it chills
returns to sunlight
and the child's leaping stitch
across the field,
bobbing above weeds
and remorse, until we go
to meet her
where she progresses,
where she rises
into the arms' reach,
her gnatty hair gleaming.

Photo by Kate ten Haken

Heather Sellers

Heather Sellers was born and raised in Orlando, Florida. Her PhD is from Florida State University, where she worked with Jerome Stern and Janet Burroway. She's an associate professor of English at Hope College. Recent work appears in the *Indiana Review*, the *Sun*, *Hawaii Review*, and *Field*.

Widow's Peak

When I would pull hairs out of it, my mother
said it's your signature, don't erase it. Okay,
I said, a sign of terrible, awesome beauty.
Well anyway better than a mole, like your
babysitter has, why your father loves those
things, I do not know. They can sprout
hairs. I didn't believe anything she told me.

She told me I inherited my widow's peak
from my grandmother, the vee of dark hair in
the center of my forehead, Frankenstein hoodlet.
Ugly-pretty, my mother always said, of plastic
flowers, sculpted shag, velvet capes, shiny black
vinyl couches and caps, my favorite things.

Last week I learned provenance of the name.
I had always thought, just below the level
of thought, in a crooked way, that the widow
part wasn't significant, it was the peak one
got with this particular hairline. The peak,
I had a peak, I was at peak, a pinnacle of beauty.

But of course the widow's peak is a sign your husband
will die and soon. Fishwives in France
turned up peaked, men drowned, and my
grandmother, my Alsace-Lorraine grandmother, lost
her husband, Buck Keating, when she was 34,
the age I will be next year. He wasn't fishing,
he wasn't in France. He was golfing at North
Shore in Wisconsin. But still. He died, she was
peaked and I have hers. I am looking
for my husband but I can see now
why he is hiding from me. Marked man.

Polar

I might just have to drown you children
I might just drown us all.
No, my brother and I said. We were blonde
and forceful then and planning
on snack, children of our own, the beach.
My mother's face was voile in
those days, and Florida was green felt
and eggshells, fingernails and rind.
Hurricanes were relaxing to me.
I thought of them as marriages.
My body was a swizzle stick. My mind a
rainy crash. You children eat a lot.
You are eating me
out of house and home. My mother's
chin was a goose. She smelled like
sweat. I pretended to be a baby when
she wasn't around. I dispersed myself
when she was. Don't ever let me hear
you say the word God, she said.
Now, she is quiet and old and fluid like a conch.
She looks out upon a bottomless lake,
Lake Underhill in Orlando, a grey lake
that refuses to reflect the sky, a pale water
that shadows what's to come. Most of the
time she doesn't remember or invent.
You two were never spanked, she says now.
I'm still falling. But I do not think in opposites.
I always knew better than that, not that.

Girlfriend

FOR ANNA LISA

What I will never forget ever is your singing in the yellow kitchen
sitting on the chair with your hands on your knees, filling up that
   kitchen
with Jubilation gospel.
That kitchen of yours had blossoms for cups, it was
the kitchen where everyone tasted like mints,
the kitchen of sun and Atlantic nights,
and our bellies were round with chocolate cake in
your kitchen with the seersucker sofa.

That night you sang a song as raw and ripe and fluttering as America.
Through the Victorian garden it shined and shrieked and struck the
   glass
roof like inverse rain,
over the brick yard, over the walls, the yews,
your voice a bamboo pole in the casual blue river of evening.

I want you to sing in every kitchen in the world!
So all the kitchens can renew themselves and run ahead like children.
If you are sleeping tonight, dragonfly. If you are wishing.
Under this moon I know you bicycle to the movies
with your own popcorn, your own script, your own personal favorite
   stars.
There are so many lives for you to fill up.

I bring you a constellation of buttons.
You turn them to notes and sing the sky.
I bring you white silk. You will sing it into a wedding,
a fluttering mountain. A famous blessing.
From the white silk you'll make a window, a flight, a third wing.
An inverse sky, a lamp for the dark small perfect world.
And a comet will take your name.

The Girl Who Would Live

The girl grew taller
when she ate nothing. Starve the
stomach, she said to her heart
and she grew one
foot that very February.
Thirteen years. She could count

the rings inside of her trunk:
loops, ridges, coiling cold,
tightening; this was growth.
She wanted to die.
We want to die suddenly.
She wanted to die

long and slowly as she had lived.
She had not lived much.
Once to the beach, where a man felt
her between her pink-white waves.
Summer. Missouri. Her cousins. The capitol.
Her white lace dress ravelled up her legs, thighs,
cotton lace a short bath of vital badnesses.

Between her legs she grew a glass of wine.
She ate her way clear of her body. She ate
as we would drink, taking in what is clear,
pleasing our throats with the thick of nothings.
Her fingernails, mucous, squares of white paper: she
chewed, swallowed. The foodless weeks hurt but the light

dizzy head, the stomach pangs so much like love;
she dove in. The delicious want that is
days and days of careful hunger
pulled her towards the center of her body.
She could push on her stomach, feel spine.
I swallowed a fish bone! She grew

sticky and ate sun. She peeled her thumb
skin, palms, feet, scalp placed swatches
of flesh on her tongue, babied these like
mint. Teased like gum. The starving shot her hair
to her waist and her legs dropped out of her waist
like quick blades. One night she was done.

Diane Seuss

Diane Seuss was raised in Niles, Michigan, and has lived in New York City and Cincinnati. Her book It *Blows You Hollow* was published in 1998 by New Issues Press. She has also published in a variety of literary magazines, including *Poetry Northwest, Third Coast, Indiana Review, Tamaqua, Primavera,* and *Exquisite Corpse.* Her work also appeared in *The PrePress Awards: Michigan Voices* and *A Loving Testimony: Remembering Loved Ones Lost to AIDS.* She was the first recipient of the Jewel Heart Poetry Prize in Ann Arbor. Seuss currently lives in Kalamazoo, Michigan, and teaches in the creative writing program at Kalamazoo College.

The Dance

It was a Moroccan restaurant.
For a celebration, the tone was sullen.
These were not heads of State, mind you,
but well-heeled people, some were moneyed,
most brilliantly educated, many steeped
in irony—let's put it this way, they all
had beautiful teeth. Not to say they were
shallow. Many were strong, some courageous.
Some had fought in wars, were marked with scars,
others had struggled for just causes, put themselves on the line
in their time, put their money where their mouth was,
stuck flowers in the barrels of guns, some
even ate crickets, in the Peace Corps, and I know
one in particular held the dying in his arms
without worrying about contagion.

There was something about the belly dancer,
however, they could not endure.
Her hair was dyed onyx, dull as a charcoal briquette,
but she had a bright blonde mustache
and her eyes were the green of pennies
which have sat for years at the bottom
of a damp jar, waiting to be spent.
She rang her finger-cymbals in the faces
of the men, inviting them to dance with her,
but they stared straight ahead,
as people will when they're being ticketed,
and the officer is lecturing them a bit,
pointing out their flaws, and it reminds them
of something shameful and parental, and they hold
themselves still, trying not to crack. Her belly-flesh
quivered, like the flank of a horse covered
in blue flies, and her costume shed sequins
and feathers. Some at the table continued to eat
in order to dissuade her.
Some glared, even waved her away.

There are many things in my life
of which I am ashamed—more than not.
But I can claim, unequivocally, that I was the one, that night,
at that table, who rose my sorry ass out of the chair
and danced with the belly dancer. I did not take her home
with me; we did not exchange phone numbers, or names.
But when she raised her arms, I raised my arms;
when she moved her hips, I moved my hips;
when she stuck out her tongue like a snake out of a basket
I stuck out my tongue. I mortified them all; I alienated
my friends, some, for good. I received her wet kisses,
one on each cheek, when the music stopped. I will not
be redeemed, I know, nor, sometimes, loved.
But when it would have been expedient not to dance,
I tell my pillow at night, *I danced.*

Kansas

If a lifetime is North America then I have reached Kansas.
From here I can see it all coming. Hail? Moving this way
from the next town, the girl has dropped all the white marbles
out of her apron. Twisters? I watch them from far off,
meandering old women bending at the waist,
berry picking. Their deep blue aprons are full
of everything that can be plucked and taken away.
Fierce gray hair flying, they can drive
a two-by-four like a golden needle through the pink silk
belly of a sow. I see Joe the Reaper, a sweet slack-jawed
boy who's too good at his work, never misses a stalk or a beat,
sweeps it all flat to the ground. Behind me, due east?
Love, its cracked voiceless bell, its proclamations and declarations,
its lobster traps, buttery pots, thwacking harpoons, its Shaker furniture,
quivering on bony legs like a newborn colt. Behind me, the restraint
of small black buckled shoes, behind me—that God. In front?
Solitude, the great desolation. Hawkish, I am
a stalked stalker. Old, with my knife, my red bowl, my funnel,
my great black apron. Alone, thirsting. In front of me is where
I will cut the arm from a cactus and finally taste the green juice
I've imagined my whole life, the wonderful thirst, the bitter quenching.
I walk, into the scribblings of sidewinders, the screeching of birds
with bloody beaks, the sun, her dress on fire, lowering herself
into the salty arms of her blue, undrinkable, moaning lover, screaming,
shaking the earth, breaking up the furniture. That God.

Houseboy

When the mailman brought your ashes I kept them on the porch for
    days.
I needed to carry the small box of you, the bones and the ash,
like a baby, in the crook of my arm, down the path of broken glass.
I needed to touch the chips and shards of you,
to scatter you, by handfuls, into water.

Instead, I hired it done—something like that.
Something like writing a check to a barefoot houseboy,
a boy in blue, pajama-like clothes, for a job well done.
He carried you for me over the broken glass.
His feet were so tough nothing could slice through them.
He hummed, half-smiling, used to doing the dirty
work for cowards with full pockets.

He scattered you, that boy. His hands and lower lip shook;
although he never met you he swallowed back his tears.
I put my arms around his thin shoulders.
I smelled his neck, the sandalwood in his clothes.
I love you I whispered, the words squeezing past the igneous
lump in my throat. I held tight, my whole body
against him, until he pushed me away
with strong, clean hands and ran,
long-limbed, disdainful and wild,
as the dead always run away from the living.

Rising

What do you after the crucifixion?
The dead body is yellowing within its cave.
What do you do with your time after the pretty one is gone?
Float in a boat, fish for compliments. Watch the blue heron pick lice
out of its wings. You can visit the memory, like a dark red
bed hemmed-in by lilacs, a sexy, lonely place, wrapping
your legs around destitute air.

Wander all you want; babble to yourself like a nun
who entered the convent to hide from grief.
Go to an apple orchard and search for the ghost
who doesn't want to be found. Around you
the world is in tremulous flower, wet, wanting to anoint the soft face
and hands of God. You can lie in the high grasses, remembering
the warm skin under your hands, the blue cotton shirt,
the pearly buttons, the clean white winding
sheet, the look in the eyes that said I *am dislodging*
myself from you, molecule by molecule...
Even now you see it all around you:
the heron opening its wings, the mist on the lake,
everything vibrating, evaporating, sparking, dissipating, rising.

Faith Shearin

Faith Shearin teaches high school English at Cranbrook Schools in Detroit. Her poems have appeared in numerous journals, including *Ploughshares*, the *Alaska Quarterly Review, New York Quarterly*, the *Charlotte Poetry Review*, and the *Chicago Review*, where she was nominated for a Pushcart Prize. She was a fellow at the Fine Arts Work Center in Provincetown and she later served on its writing committee. She was the Writer-in-Residence at the Interlochen Arts Academy in 1996.

Entropy

My mother's kitchen was asleep.
Our family didn't gather there—
we lived and ate in our bedrooms—
hypnotized by the blue lights of T.V.
But, in her kitchen, pots and pans
floated, belly up, in the week-old
water, and our garbage, smiling,
outgrew its bag. All of this very

slowly, as if in a dream. My mother
despises what can never truly
be done so she does not care for cooking
or cleaning. If one cooks a fine dinner
one must wash the dishes to cook
a fine breakfast to wash the dishes
to cook a fine lunch and so on. My mother
explained this one afternoon in the basement
where the laundry grew around us like trees.

Our jungle-home was a metaphor for
my mother giving in to entropy.
When wine spilled on the couch and we
laughed as the stain unfurled,
we were embracing chaos. When we
fell asleep with the lights on
and the T.V. talking, we were
the weeds in our own garden.

My mother's kitchen was haunted.
Her refrigerator leaned to one
side and made only brown ice.
Her biscuits were flat as plates.
But none of this mattered because
we were forgetting ourselves
even as we were becoming ourselves.
We pursued truth, beauty,

the meaning of life—while
my mother's kitchen discovered
decay. All this unravelling—
the moldy food, the newspapers
piling up to the ceiling.
We loved each other like that:
bananas going black on the counter,
lines coming in around our eyes.

Desire

The act of standing, penniless, in a store
where one might buy the porcelain skin
of beauty, the hot flowers of love, or glasses
so strong they see the other side of death.
The moment when a lover's mouth begins its
descent into flesh: a butterfly into forest.

Luck

Beneath the suburbs is a place to be late and wrong.
Plain and unlucky, I have visited many times.
Some days I feel a sinking towards that land
of blunders and my shirt turns to polyester,

my laugh goes so sharp it breaks bones. The first
time was a Halloween I spent with a distant cousin.
He is always in that under place: so drab even
mosquitoes overlook him. We spent the night

beside a silent phone, dressed as eggs, our hands
folded like bad cards. Once you've been under,
something shifts; you always go back. In recent years
I have gone there to miss trains, read maps

backwards, pay the rent twice and starve.
Sometimes I'm moving down a perfectly flat sidewalk
and falling. Once you've been, the other losers
are obvious: you see them knocking over

glass figurines, describing oral sex to the man
who cleans their teeth. They invite ten to dinner
and find themselves chewing alone. In a crowd
the unlucky throw the lucky off-balance,

everyone's feet begin to squeak. When I was small
I loved a girl who gathered light by breathing;
her mouth was warm as sleep. Sitting close,
I would glow from looking at her, borrow shine

like a moon. My mother once explained:
we can't all be beautiful; even a gaunt field
feels the cold kiss of morning.

Ruins

The first one was in Michigan and I loved him
    like I was digging in a foreign land and he was
        the ruin I came to discover. Michigan is as cold

as people imagine and when I remember him now
    he is leaned against one of those gaudy American
        cars, big as boats, and all but his face is lost

in layers. This was a campus full of kids in knickers
    and baby blue sweaters who, when they laughed, shielded
        their mouths with mittened hands. I longed to uncover

flesh the same way I longed to uncover earth in a place
    where winter long outstayed its welcome. I wanted
        my beauty, whatever it was, held up to my blind eye

and described; I thought loving was the same as
    sifting down through ash to find Pompeii. In Michigan
        there were layers of snow and layers of clothing

and with that first boy it was as if I kept undressing
    until I was naked but I found a way, that young, to take
        off more. Down in the dirt of each other every clue we

uncovered was not enough. The snow did not stop falling
    and now, a decade later, there is the shape of him outlined
        again and again until he is larger but less detailed:
            a relic from the ancient landscape explaining me.

Matrimony

When I went to visit I was, for one week, his wife.
The house was small and well formed like it might
belong to a doll. Mornings, he went to work and, while
he was gone, I walked from room to room in search of
my brain. There was a dog that longed to be walked
or fed and most days I ignored him the same way

I ignored myself. On the third day, I had a fever
and I could feel that any word I might utter would
lose its meaning. At first I had been a fine wife—
spotless dishes, low-cut dresses—but I was shrinking
and soon I would not matter as much as the dog.

Whenever the phone rang it was not for me
and when the plumber came to fix the sink he asked
if my parents were home. Luckily, my husband came
back from his long day and uttered the words
"comfort" and "reason." He did not notice my small
voice or my boiled head and we smiled and smiled

like we wanted to blind one another with sharp
white light. I imagined I could try on wife like
a fake fur coat and the way I looked in it would
make me laugh. Instead, wife was like gaining
fifty pounds, all on my ass, or waiting for bad news

from a doctor. When a person pretends marriage
they are brought in from the wild and placed naked
in a cement cell. A popcorn-crunching crowd comes
close and stares. On the plane home I was served
dinner for one and, afterwards, my tray table stayed
in the forward and upright position. I found my brain:
on my head all along like a useless pair of glasses.

Photo by Carole Steinberg Berk

Marc J. Sheehan

Marc J. Sheehan was born in Grand Rapids, Michigan, in 1954. He earned his MFA degree in writing from the University of Michigan. His collection of poems, *Greatest Hits,* was published by New Issues Press in 1998. His poetry, fiction, and essays have appeared in such journals as *Michigan Quarterly Review, Pennsylvania Review, New York Quarterly,* and others. He has been awarded grants from the National Endowment for the Arts and the Michigan Council for the Arts.

Thanksgiving

The question as always is just how close
to the headwaters we have to trace a thing,
as when the wounded deer staggered in to
a shallow bend of the Coldwater River
just as we were getting ready to meet
my sister's new partner who ended up
wading in past two failed marriages,
her flirtations with petty theft, a car crash,
unlettered disappearances, and now
a Thanksgiving dinner being kept warm
and a Lions game flickering away
in an empty living room, so he could put
the deer out of its suffering with one
well-aimed blow of a short-handled, twelve pound
sledge hammer to its antlerless head,
as well as to convince us by the way
he did this smoothly without spooking the doe
or having to repeatedly hammer
the animal until it crumpled so we
could drag it out of the freezing water,
that beneath his shy thick-handedness here
at last was a man who could handle a heart's
unforeseen turns and plunges over stones.

The Off Season

The summer homes have been closed and shuttered.
The fish house is a faint smell and a sign
for smoked Coho and next spring's charter boats.
The fishwife looks so disconcertingly like
an old lover that for a moment you think
about staying to see Lake Michigan freeze.
The cement fountain is drained and filled
with dry leaves whose color the last tour of
tourists took back with them downstate in snapshots.
In the Family Tavern old men complain
about the weather, lost love and strawberries.
There are shiny new CD's in the jukebox
(no one plays them), and pickled eggs on the bar.
There's a final concert at the opera house—
restored with money from the Arts Council—
but it's local folks playing for relatives.
Some of the summer places are mansions,
though most are clapboard boxes. Either way
if home is where you write the rent check, then
you settle for the local bed and breakfast.
Even with the cut in rates they've thrown in
an extra helping of silence and all
the longing you can stand to bring back for free.

The Wine Spectator

Because my sun sign, my moon sign
and half my planets are in Scorpio,
because I paid a full day's

wages to a woman to find this out,
and because I'm at Partners in Wine
buying for a writer's signing

party at the bookstore I work for,
I'm especially attentive when
a biker with "Scorpions" emblazoned

on the back of his black leather jacket
(as well as a patch
with *Detroit* embroidered on it)

asks about California chardonnays.
He has chrome chains and iron
crosses adorning his jacket's flaps;

he has Harley Davidson's
mean eagle sewn over
his left breast pocket.

He thinks the vintner might be Rodney
Strong, but he's not sure.
He strokes his black goatee and seems

too polite to point out to the tight-lipped
sales clerk how little help he's being.
After the biker says good-bye,

I decide finally on white and buy a case
of a Chilean blend after
the clerk says the wine is nicely

balanced.

Angora

Jeff snaps the electric scissors to life
and starts underneath, around a goat's penis,
then down its legs, revealing front knees
callused from unreligious kneeling.
Then comes hog-tying to shear sides and back,
and at last he trims the fine angelic hair
grown long over almost human eyes.
Afterwards, the rams rear back and butt heads
to see who in their new skin will be king.
You will say men are just like that.
Still, in good times you can get someone to buy
even hair from the belly stained with urine
which would turn golden if it were rinsed out.
Maybe by next spring things will improve—
more kids, less blood, a blade that doesn't dull,
someone to alchemize this pile of foul wool,
now filling one large size brown paper bag.

Second Marriage

They wake in the room above the chapel
which this time around is their living room—
the flower girl and ring bearer still
asleep in their adjoining pastel sanctums
dreaming of their various parents.
Somewhere the best man is dressed to kill,
crouched beneath a stark maple this first day
of deer season—gray morning of low clouds.
At home the maid of honor pads cold
linoleum and laces coffee with scotch.
Last night the bride wondered into sleep
over whether to wear her first wedding gown,
or the blue of her best friend's betrothal.
The groom knows that by the time the honeymoon
has waned the Catholics will already
have resurrected their chipped nativity,
making him think back to removing the claws
from his neighbor's old bathtub to halo
the Madonna she planted in her back yard.
They know now there are partings before death.
They suspect that winning tickets and health
would be better than *for poorer* and croup.
Still, they have new rings and a baby sitter
so they can spend the weekend in Pentwater.
They have fifths of whiskey, liters of soda
and a refrigerator which is lit
from within by huge bowls of coleslaw.
They will have the instant memory of photographs
that develop by themselves, and cake
layered with icing and topped by plastic bells.
The minister will ask if anyone objects and tell
the groom that he needn't slip him that fifty.
But they couldn't get a plumber for that much
and besides, the groom knows how to fix almost
anything he can work a wrench around.
And what he doesn't know he is determined
this time to figure out, or live with broke.

Joseph Sheltraw

Joseph Sheltraw was born and raised in Saginaw, Michigan, and has lived in the Great Lakes state for most of his life. He earned a BS in liberal arts from Central Michigan University in 1989. In 1993, he earned an MFA in creative writing and an MA in literature from Western Michigan University. He has published both fiction and poetry in *Witness, Colorado Review, Quarterly West, Sou'wester,* and *Sycamore Review.* Currently, he lives in the Detroit area and teaches part-time at Oakland University.

The White Kid

Don't think that the tall white kid
among us doesn't have power,
his hair not stubbled but feathered,
his mouth not orange and thick but thin,
and nose not pushed-in but long and narrow.

Every Friday, pouring in from the cities,
we frighten you, except for the white kid
we keep as your mascot, elongated bone,
two eyes green as stones.
His arms smell like chalk.
A referee walks by, a lattice of fingers
keeping the ball away
until the white kid comes and releases it,

but he doesn't release it, not this time,
and the ball is thrown anyway
and this room with the creaky floorboards
is alive with our running, our cadence,
our drills of balance and correspondence—
yes, and there's snow outside.
Fresh snow. White sweat against
the slabs of car windows.

One of you screams:
"Does it rub off?" Our answer is yes.
Yes it does! Look at the white kid
who worships our tight flanks,
imagines our skins permeable
as the snow that lends you water.
Look at him blush—all eyes
and floppy hair. And there's
such grace in the way he shouts,
fingers the outline of his mouth.
The way he sings, urges us to win,
recites each of our dreams
as we spread rage across the gym.

Carnival Worker

He was far outside the fairgrounds, beyond
the tents collapsing like parachutes,
beyond the Tilt-a-Whirl and the Big Bopper, beyond
the little kids who teased him, their tongues
snapping like miniature turtles. I have
a photograph of him, licking his cigarette paper
on the beach of Atlantic City,
letting the tobacco stick to his chin,
while Mom is waving in front of him,
determined to ignore his advances.
He tried pinching my boobs, she told me later.
Pops was in the john, forklifting his arms into
the gaze of a mirror, hoping to impress the broad
outside. Mom's friend, the one
with the camera, told the guy to smile.
He didn't. Until that moment, he didn't even
acknowledge the existence of film, or
the existence of the lazy surf behind
him, pulling his hair. He just rode in
on some ferriswheel, the lighted spindles
carrying him until he saw these
two women in cut-off shorts,
drunk as dogs, waiting to be tugged
away, at the last moment, outside the frame.
I don't know why his left eye looks dead,
why he looks down into the sand
when she take the picture, why
his fly is open, why his right cheek is scarred,
why his t-shirt is stained with what looks like blood.
I don't know why my mother and her friend
talked to him, why she lied about him to my father,
why she made excuses about offering him a drink, why
she later said he looked burly, kind of handsome
in a Burt Lancaster sort of way, why,
after all these years, I keep his picture
in my wallet, behind my driver's license.

Boys in Boxing Poses

The way we stand you can tell this isn't serious
but our brothers are there and these girls stand
inconspicuously on porches, biting fingernails,
hoping for blood. It's like swimming, and so
I'm swimming as I lift my chin, shove
my hands forward. Before I know it
I'm dreaming up ways my skin can talk, letting myself
tumble through the various hyacinths behind the garage.
Seven hours of detention with this shit.
I swear to God when he pointed at me I was Achilles
before the fortress of Troy, armor chipped,
ready to burn, but when he hit me
with that roundhouse left, my body plummeted,
buckling against the crabapples my father planted
the year before. In a few days, he will forget me,
move onto more challenging conquests:
Candy Abunkovicz' bra, Donnie C's water bong.
On this block names are dead as trees,
lost amid the cities we only dream about.
This boy over me is my only furnace for love.
When he knocks me over the porch steps,
I want to kiss him as if he were a photograph
put down beside a fireplace, or a framed
painting in a museum. When he leans into my chest,
his hands grappling me like meat hooks,
I run my eyes all over him, put my face between
his heavy lock of arms and begin to breathe.

Epilogues from Seven Unsuccessful Stories about My Father

I

As I descend into the pit, where my father begins each day pouring liquid fire into the mouths of sand molds, I see engine blocks, pockmarked and desolate: V6's, V8's, rows of them huddled together like dead bodies. Beside them, Father points out the bits and spears of leftover metal on the floor, tiny iron stems that look like blackened bluets or soybean roots.

II

I love the power of this place. The corrugated walls have scorch marks, red-haired streaks that rise up from the dirt and touch the massive ladles above. At night, days later, I'll dream I'm gliding around in these ladles, white hot metal coming to greet me as I float above the precious hell: Hands strapped against the control panel. Each finger charged with a sense of purpose, each rivet below me red-faced and bursting, squinting to be known.

III

The rest of the men have their sons too, and like gods we sneak into the cafeteria and devour the battered shapes before us: Doritos, Hershey bars, cans of Coke. Afterwards we walk around the plant and pass people with silvery suits, slip by the men's room with the strange missing door, salute the 20¢ coffee machine. Father grasps my hand and whispers, 'Don't remember this. Remember the ballgames, the picnics, the way your mother moves through a room. But don't remember this.'

IV

On the drive back home, the river next to us is large and slovenly, long shadows of clouds engulf us and leave. When we pull into a Seven-Eleven for slurpees, I think how he comes home each night with blisters, fingers like swollen carrots, orange and gnarled, which Mother kisses and handles like a basket of strange fruit.

V

When I'm nineteen and just kicked out of Jesuit school, I come back home and deliver secrets to my family. Wonderful secrets, a language which I know Father acquired in the middle of the night when he wanted to wash himself clean. Voices peering through blinds, little hand voices that squeak timidly through the bedroom windows and say: *Come. Come on over here, see what's outside.*

VI

Months pass before I go to church again and pray. Murals above the altar will show cherubims lancing the hearts of devils, some bodies stoned, some with tongues cut out. Men like my father pass collection plates and begin the slow rise of dreams, the sad-faced motion that every man has cherished. By then, I will have discovered that each life has a freshness and each man nudges his flower toward the next wonderful escape.

VII

Later, when I'm married and have kids of my own, he comes home again: a pair of ropy arms, a scruffy neck. Standing inside the kitchen next to Mom, I watch him eat. I look at the careful way he handles a coffee mug. I look at those hands and think how much desire was squeezed through the slag, how much weight each passing dream had before it hit the fires.

Photo by Severn Thomas

F. Richard Thomas

F. Richard Thomas is professor of American Thought and Language at Michigan State University and editor of Years Press. In addition to six chapbooks of poems, his publications include *Frog Praises Night: Poems with Commentary* (Southern Illinois University Press); a novel, *Prism: The Journal of John Fish*; and a book on the relationship of poetry to photography, *Literary Admirers of Alfred Stieglitz*. He is also editor of *Americans in Denmark: Comparisons of the Two Cultures by Writers, Artists, and Teachers* and *The Landlocked Heart: Poems from Indiana*. He has received a Michigan Council for the Arts Award and two Fulbright Awards to teach in Denmark. A full-length book of poetry, *Death at Camp Pahoka*, will be published by Michigan State University Press in 2000.

The Last Cherry Bomb

At the backyard party,
after blossoming of sparklers,
after bottle rockets burned bright pistils into the stars
and darkness flowed over us again like the sure course of blood to the
    heart,
I prepared a grand Independence Day finalé:
I'd blow the seams off a 30 gallon garbage can,
blast the lid off in a mushroom of smoke,
frighten the unsuspecting kids,
and deafen the other adults into a stupor of memory—
the America that used to be,
when M-80's and cherry bombs were more fun than dangerous.

Oh, sure, as kids, we'd heard of fireworks at the ballpark gone awry,
but only parents knew someone who lost an eye, perhaps,
or several fingers on the fourth of July.
Not someone we ever knew.
No.
This year, I'd take us back
to see if we could savor what we lost.

So I lit the 30-year-old sand-textured bomb and ran and waited.
But all we got was a flat fup and a small white puff.
My gallery burst the silence with their laughs,
squeaked back and forth in aluminum lawnchairs,
chortled and guffawed,
Their kids looked at each other, raised their eyebrows,
wondered what was funny to their crazed agéd parents.

Then I laughed, too—
laughed
at this failure of violence
in the backyard of our treelined street in our small town,
where city lights had only slightly dimmed the stars,
and chirp and creak of tree frogs and crickets rolled over us like fog
or sparkler smoke,
while much of the cherry-bombless-world beyond,
a fiction we barely understood,
roiled like an aneurysm
in the deep arteries of the night.

What Opens

"When the sperm cells obediently arrive in the vicinity of
the calling egg . . . molecules on the egg's surface may cast
out a kind of fishing line, hook the sperm, and reel it in."

Shadows of Forgotten Ancestors, Sagan and Druyan (309).

When you arrive at the pinnacle of a mountain in Spain
that overlooks the Mediterranean,
you tremble, where the air is thin;
your heart knocks in your throat like Death
and long fingers of wind dance down the mountains from Granada,
ruffle the hair on the back of the head,
caress the ancient terraces,
lift the hem of the sea's silk dress,
and you have no choice:
a door opens to Yes,
a tongue from the far side hooks you,
reels you in.
You enter—undone, transformed, possessed.

    ~

Before the closed door, when the bolt slips in the catch,
when the hinge sighs,
and a sudden inspiration,
   like a soft gasp,
greets you at the threshold,
do not resist.
Pass over.

Death at Camp Pahoka

"It is *choice* that decides which of the quantum worlds we measure in our experiments, and therefore which one we inhabit."

John Gribbin

Kitchen crew,
rinse boy,
I dipped each plate
into the large stone sink of hot water
till garbage floated inches deep.
Under the surface
my hand seemed to slither
through intestines and the tails of dead rats.
One evening after mess,
nauseated by the steaming tubs of slime,
I staggered to my tent,
doubling over in the pine grove,
holding my gut until I collapsed on my cot.
The last I remember is the smell of tarp,
sweat trickling in the hair around my ears,
the whine of cicadas,
a centipede crawling across the shadows of leaves
that lay, scarcely moving, on the yellow canvas roof.

~

I'm sure I died that day
and woke into a different world,
a different kitchen,
where the kid who scraped the plates before I rinsed,
said he, like me, had never been away from home.
Though slop still filled the sink,
the pine grove stood more green and
stars more brilliant
above the Mess Hall.
   I wonder if an In Memoriam plaque
now hangs above that other sink—
"One more Boy Scout, First Class, Rinse boy,

killed by swill."
But even more,
I wonder how I knew to choose this universe:
this charmed one,
this one with this daughter
to whom I pass each dish to dry,
who gives it to my son to put away
then snaps his butt with her towel,
this wife who wipes the table clean,
this life.

Joining Hands

i

Predictably
I did not predict
the way the moonlight lifts your belly
into music.

This dream that we live
has a mind of its own.

ii

Often I think God does not matter.

While you sleep,
your diary spreads open over your heart.
Some words seep over your breasts
and trickle down your stomach.

This matters.

iii

When the red
split-leaf maple in the yard
blossoms in the iris of your opening eye,
I am astonished.

iv

Suddenly,

in the middle of speechlessness,
we become moon and bone,
the language that should not be spoken
when we are like this,
silent and spacious poem.

v

As the eagle's wings bewitch the wind's strength,
so our breathing becomes us.

vi

As the diving eagle relinquishes the wind,
so our breathlessness becomes us.

vii

Sometimes we lie together
as quietly as the grass.

Then how we love
to feel the wind running through us!

viii

No, it's not
the skin around our eyes
creasing deeper with age,
it's the light around our faces
becoming more intense,
as we move closer to the front of the stage,
joining hands for a bow.

ix

We write
like we love,
as if,
in these bodies,
we could.

A grouping of poems inspired by Coleman Barks' translations of Rumi. *F.R.T.*

Richard Tillinghast

Richard Tillinghast is the author of six books of poetry and a memoir of Robert Lowell. His most recent poetry collections are *The Stonecutter's Hand* (David R. Godine, 1995) and *Today in the Cafe Trieste* (1997), new and selected poems issued by Salmon Publishing in Ireland. In 1997 he edited *A Visit to the Gallery,* a collection of poems written in response to paintings at the Museum of Art at the University of Michigan. For the past twenty years he has reviewed new poetry for the *New York Times Book Review;* he also reviews and writes literary essays for the *Wall Street Journal* and the *New Criterion,* as well as writing travel articles for the *Times.* A faculty member in the MFA program at the University of Michigan since its inception in 1984, he also teaches at The Poet's House in Ireland.

Father in October

FOR BROWNIE AND KATE

When the smell of freshly sharpened pencils had lost
Its power to intoxicate, when our first
Infatuation with September had slackened—
With its satchels and homework and new teacher;
When the leaves of the late-blooming chrysanthemums
In our frost-finished back garden had blackened,
One morning my mother would retrieve our winter
Hats and scarves, our gloves and heavy raingear.
My father would go up attic, bring down the storms
And snug them in, between ourselves and the weather.

One hundred years of our family had lived
Beneath that house's airy ceilings, had sat
By a grate where coal sputtered and glowed in the glass
Cases where my grandfather's books were shelved—
Shakespeare, the Brontës, Dickens, Sir Walter Scott.
And the house told stories, of interest only to us:
The well, sealed after Uncle John drowned a cat.
The deep-cut initials my older brother carved
Above the stairs. The bed my mother was born in.
Every dip in the floorboards spoke, every curious stain

Remembered. To marry my mother, my father found
In 1932, was to husband her house.
Its *fin de siècle* wiring was a fireman's nightmare;
What was airy in June was drafty in December.
"Manage," "Simplify," his granite New England
Eyes said. Those Willifords must have seemed another
Species altogether—with their Southernness,
Their leaky roof, their Eastlake furniture.
There was hardly a marble-topped table that didn't wobble,
Or a chair that couldn't have used some glue or a nail.

Saturdays he'd be up by six. First
A shave, and with his shaving brush he'd soap
Clean the lenses of his gold-rimmed glasses.
Then he'd collect himself over coffee and make a list,
Numbered and neat, of his day's projects in the shop
He had built out back under the hickory trees.
A nimbus of sawdust surrounding his concentration,
He'd turn a chair-leg on his lathe, cut out
A bracket or brace with his jigsaw, then fashion
A toy pistol for me, or a paddle-wheel boat.

Daddy's real work was engineering. His own
Dreams and epiphanies came to him, I imagine,
In the language of his calling—straightedged and clear
As a blueprint, verifiable by time and motion
Studies. His few inventions that made a profit,
The many he drew in his mind but had to give
Up on, lived a life pristine and platonic—
Not subject to half-measures or the change of season,
Not battered by weather or in need of repair
Like the mortal house I judged him master of.

His Days

When one of his black moods bedeviled him,
When the wince of some remembered pain—
Some wrong done to him, some cruelty of his own—
Hurt him like a surge melting down
Bad wiring, what choice was left to him
But to flinch and swallow and bear it like a man?

The cottage's slates and silences became
His kingdom, its weathers his own. He would coax
To a blaze coal and turfs each morning, and chunks
Of beech he split with his own axe.
The farmer's son or Sunday hikers would see him
Hunched at his kitchen table, away in his books.

Then obscurely one morning he'd lock his cottage door.
With a word to no one he'd be gone,
To look at an old church somewhere, or the ruin
Of a tower down a dirt track, or a stone
Incised with markings no one could decipher,
Its language crumbling by degrees in the rain.

He could navigate the old script. And he knew why an arch
Was rounded or gothic. Why the mermaid
Held a mirror. Which sins the monks allowed
Themselves, and which they disavowed.
He knew the griefs of the high kings, belonged to the church
Of bitterness, had bet on the cards of pride.

But when on some grimy market town's main street
He heard a child, eyes widening in wonder,
Call out "Daddy!", reaching for its father,
It cut him like the crack of leather.
Then, it seemed, the pain was complete.
The water was wide, and he could not swim over.

A Morning

Knowing the answer or not
knowing the answer,
penciling the morning in,
staring right back at the egg yolks
while the baby crawls on the rug.
Watching the last day of August
transpire, with its sharp, peculiar light.

Working for the department, changing
a tire, letting the phone ring.
Innocent, truly not knowing
the answer,
honestly holding no opinion.
Seventy-four degrees exactly.

The ordinariness of it,
I suppose, was what struck the Buddha,
camped out along the road to awakening
as he watched the moment ignite,
incinerate, and disperse.

Tea

Erase a statue of Buddha, eyes lidded on nonexistence.
Erase topiary.
Take away red paint and gilding if you can.

This is a place to sit for a while,
the mats fresh,
smell of rain in rushes.

A crane glides without moving its wings
over the stream's length.
Peonies bloom in silk.

Is the stream a part of nature, or has it been
altered by the sages?
A shower blows up among cypresses up trail.

The tea master is away.
Otherwise how should I be here?

Over foothills scrolling,
mist brightens and evanesces.
Families of monkeys move over the ridge above,
through jungle, mist frozen on their muzzles.

Brown smoke from cooking fires
finds a path up here
from where the nomads camp.
God knows what they are burning.

Then the clear green tea:
green like water at the bottom of the ocean,
but hot as a bowl of soup.

Behind us, the trek over the mountains,
hand-drawn maps, bad knees and brambles.

Who knows what thundery warlord or dakini
caused the wind to blow the clouds
from one side of the mountain to the other?

Where the trail switchbacks above us,
two immortals play at chess.

Rodney Torreson

Rodney Torreson (b. 1951) grew up on a farm in Iowa and currently lives in Grand Rapids. His book, *A Ripening of Pinstripes: Called Shots on the New York Yankees,* was issued in 1998. A chapbook, *On a Moonstruck Gravel Road,* appeared in 1994.

When the Babe Stormed New York

the snows burned brighter.
Subways rose on a rail of wind.
They merged on some dizzy parallel
with elevated trains,
leaving trails of floss,
as the two crisscrossed over city blocks
which the Babe blew past
in a cream-colored car,
banishing great Manhattan shadows,
while on his way to a Bronxville flat.
There he'd needle the Victrola,
nuzzle Flora's back,
as she giggled and squirmed
into the Babe's arms
from lonely outer reaches of her love seat.

When the Babe stormed New York,
he lit up every jittering nightclub.
They swelled and throbbed gloriously
the moment Babe, in a camel-hair coat,
stepped into the foyer.
It was God's blessing that the war was over.
The whole town smoked like those three cigars
Babe puffed at one time
in a show window of a cigar factory in Boston,
the Babe so big he throttled prohibition,
who died to his appetites every night
and in that forgiving hour before the game
was rubbed back to his body.

When the Babe stormed New York,
police began to believe in their nightsticks
like never before, and everyone was safe.
Babe left Flora behind at her door,
necking with the new fur
he bought her, while he'd go God-knows-where.

Babe waved a kiss
that didn't miss anybody, and the last
of those great firedogs sniffed
out the smoke of passion
and his nostrils flared,
and fans forgot they'd all be dead
in a hundred years.

Wooden Ducks

My father's chisel skims them
close to breathing, who know
the pond of piano top
and shelf, their breath outside them,
given off by trees and seaweed
in their slow emission. In no hurry
the breath plays at windows of the house,
one day sweeping through in gusts—
or the wild heart,
born when a foot steps on a leaf,
drafts beneath the door.

Sometimes we long to be like that,
come to our body
as if we were never born
and meet ourselves in perfect wooden sleep,
behind us our poor unattached wings,
those backs of chairs,
which despite their
feathery spokes and spools do not
give us rise. But knowing this we glory
how in our flying breath
we settle there within ourselves,
while a duck slips from
the carver's hand, bobbing, nodding,
and our chiseled eyes awaken
in the wind.

Ties

Out on the prairie a few string ties remain:
restless chopsticks
in search of a Chinese western.
And there are bow ties, those butterflies,
that will have its man
hovering among flowers,
but will keep him cold in the conference room,
never flying out to bring back
a leaf vision of lake or loon.

But most are long ties which knot
at the throat and take one to church
and insist on proper theologies,
ties that pull one down the straight road,
bind one tightly to the law,
themselves leading a double life,
secretly dipping into spaghetti or soup.

There are ties that relax in the late afternoon
when the man finally says
to hell with this life
and he pulls the tie loose,
that spend time in libraries
tracing their awful roots back to bibs
worn by enlightened Neanderthals.
Somewhere Stanley Laurel's tie wipes a tear.
Oliver Hardy's waves bye-bye.
Oh what a sacrilege declares
the long faced council of ties,
who all day add numbers
but never figure out why
they try so hard for a cutting edge.

There are ties that make the wearer measure up
from his first glance
at himself in the mirror,
and ties that will turn upside down
and hang a man from the rafters
of his garage when he fails.

Maris and Dylan Came Scowling out of Hibbing, Minnesota

This town boasts the world's largest hole
and it bore through both of them.
Each had what the other did not,
traits stuffed, overgrown,
as if in the forty years that Hibbing moved south
and the Hull-Rust pit encroached,
things got mixed up: scent of dogs, mail routes;
gene pools split on couch, banister, and branch,
entering leaf buds
and x and y fell from the alphabet
or scored in throng.

Maris born for Pat Boone shoes
but no Pat smile, shoulders of the Mesabi range
while Dylan was born
in Hibbing at age six,
for leather jacket and boots,
and ducktail, no shoulders, but a shrug.
One turned toward bang, one hum.
And at Tiger Stadium,
before Maris hit his fifty-eighth home run,
he leaned against his bat
and watched Canadian geese,
one large flock fly over;
it was the melting down of stone age man;
it was the sixties being born.
Dylan, born when his old self moved in from Duluth,
likely made concoctions in the pit
as boys are apt to do
whenever a fence's law breaks down.
When cells dislodged
as old Hibbing was overturned,
they came alive in contact with his skin
and each fish mouth nibbled a way in.

When Maris had looked up,
something deeper than home runs
held him like the white band does
across the goose's throat.
He squinted at the v-shape,
he who hated travel
from Kansas City to New York,
who made this leap because of Dylan
(Dylan's leaps were good for two)
who was nurtured in this soil
where houses, churches, saloons and stores
leaped each other for those forty years.

Maris stood outside the batter's box,
put off the cunning in this world,
put off the frowning Terry Fox, and Dylan wailed,
"I leap to Selma and Viet Nam,
I leap into the veins of leaves,
I leap into chlorophyll,
I leap into the mountain goat's horns
and turn them upside down."

Then Maris saw Hibbing as a shell-shocked town,
the courthouse crumbling, its windows blown.
And before he stepped in and hit the ball
into the upper deck in right,
just below where the geese had flown,
he glimpsed Dylan's myopic vision,
everything from Saigon to Hibbing
blurred into one,
and Maris leaped over gender
to a place where Dylan
raised ore dust in his throat and sang
and Maris tempered his distrust of the fans
in a place just the other side of music.

Photo by Deb Meijer

Robert VanderMolen

Robert VanderMolen lives and works as a house painter in Grand Rapids (where he was born in 1947). His most recent collection of poetry, *Peaches*, appeared in 1998. Other works include *Of Pines, Night Weather, Circumstances*, and *Along the River*. He received an NEA Fellowship in 1995. His poems have appeared in *Grand Street, Sulfur, Epoch, Mudfish, Artful Dodge, House Organ*, and *Parnassus* in recent years.

In February

I used to come home
From the foundry at night
Drink a beer
And fall asleep on the couch

Kathy thought I was sexy
Covered with grime

I lost count
Of my mornings

    The trick, he insisted,
Is to be clever
Without seeming clever

I thought that made sense

But I would have to learn
To relax when I answered the phone

    My Dad said,
Much of what we know
About history
Has to do with warfare

Can't argue with that.
Still,
When you look
At stars from the park at night
You prefer they stay put

That is, no matter where you travel
You want things to stay
Familiar behind you

Outside of Town

1

Lou Gehrig's disease
Is caused by bad diet
And drinking diet pop,
She said, at the next table

With a grey sky
Melting over the windows
Like bankruptcy

2

Spring training
In Florida,
Pulled stomach muscles,
Stolen wallet and clothes—

A red truck
In a field of disappointment

The staghorn tufts of sumac
Battered by birds and weather

I told you, she said,
Tax time is no time
To be hiring

Life goes on, her male friend noted

Some are lucky to be lucky,
She said finally,
Standing, fooling in her purse

Painting Shutters

A woman unloading
Her station-wagon

Bobbed hair, a white blouse
I'm not sure

I saw her face
Even her hands

But her skirt
Was tight and black

She moved
Like someone I knew once.

Waiting everyday

Fixing martinis,
Sweeping the floor

Sitting in front of the door
Where palms skipped about

On the boulevard. Such traffic,
All those voices in Spanish

Bodies

This boy came into the library,
Said there was a body
In the river.
I didn't just fall off
A turnip truck, she said.
Being originally from Saginaw
Or Bad Ax . . .
One cold front following another
Week after week,
The weatherman answers his door
With a pistol stuck in the elastic
Of his jogging pants.
I know a drunk when I sleep
With one, she continued.
He used to ski too
Until the cold got him.
But he wasn't no suicide.
Not in his family. They like to fight.
The attorney removed his glasses,
The older you get
The worse you look without money.
On TV a documentary
Pointed out that ancient columns
Were modeled on tree trunks.
Maybe they ran out
Of large trees. I don't know,
She said, everytime you get one thing
Figured out . . .

Miles Davis

That period before visitors
When the light hums overhead.

You dissolve,
No one to answer to

An hour, a day, a week.
The light, the door . . .

Into a private scent

Just as it was meant to be.

Except nothing
Is the same or exactly true.

What visitors
Are we talking about?

Making a Fire

    Sitting on a raw stump
Your bottom is sore with frost.

The truck won't start.
There is however a beauty in cold.
This absolutism, this precision, this Germanism.
It brings to mind flannel sheets.
Widows in their 40s,
Calendar pictures
Of maples in snow, fir and beech.
Yellow birch leaning
At edges of ponds, ice radiating . . .

    Warm tub, a leaded glass of brandy,
Her hand reaching towards you

A sort of coaxing

Photo by Diane Wakoski

Diane Wakoski

Diane Wakoski, who is Writer-in-Residence and University Distinguished Professor at Michigan State University, where she has taught for more than twenty years, is a native of southern California. She has published many collections of poetry, including *The Motorcycle Betrayal Poems* (Simon & Schuster, 1971) and *Emerald Ice* (Black Sparrow Press, 1989), which won the William Carlos Williams Prize from the PSA. Her current project is an epic poem of the West, *The Archaeology of Movies and Books,* the most recent volume of which was published in 1998.

Blue Nails

Hands as little as the leaves of the sapling Honey Locust Tree,
and he looks at them as if he knows how
they would feel, landing kitten-like on his shoulders.
With her small fingernails painted light blue
and looking pagan to me,
as if she worshipped Oak Trees
and spoke only superstitions,
she reaches out to offer me a piece of paper
and the little blue nails
are like bits of broken eggshell,
tumbled among the departing leaves.
He has given her
everything he can, even spreading his arms out
wide, imitating crucifixion,
and she imagines that he's a scarecrow
standing there with her in a roadside park,
next to a local cornfield,
where they've stopped the car to smoke
and talk. Her little blue nails
must not look like anything the movies ever
offered as seductive, and her smoking hands not like
those of a Patricia Neal in *The Fountainhead,* but like
a kindergartner's hands, decorated with the glitter of broken robin's egg
shells. Yet those are the nailed hands
he'd like to hold in his own hands,
gather to him,
build something with them.
But right now, there he is, yes
he's the one, nailed
to the cross of her pagan nature, wispy, dancing
over the marsh in a blue flame, he transfixed,
nailed there in love with her little
blue nails. Her hands,
she says, belong to another
man.

Of course, I find that
very hard to believe. Why, if that other love weren't dead
would she
paint her fingernails
blue? Broken eggshell
blue?

Costa Rican Coffee

I scissor open the brown and white pack
and instantly the smell of morning
fills this kitchen. The steaming water drips through
the maker like a lover moving next
to your sleeping body in the night and putting an
arm around your torso so that you feel as if
your body is as beautiful as the Venus de Milo. How lucky
you are in this loveless world
to have a cup of coffee to start the day,
its brown tongue presses against your lips
until you feel their redness.
You aren't in a movie, you aren't
rich or happy, you aren't
even doing something meaningful with your life. It's just
a new day and you remember that
the arms which held you
during the night
have been missing for centuries.
You know
nothingness;
smell and taste its
topaz mouth.

Wanting Bees

You are writing your
autobiography and
asking me to buy a copy. You sent an
order form in the mail.

But in the same letter
you said
you were tired of hearing
my decadent descriptions of soft-shelled crabs
eaten in New Jersey, or a blueberry tart
I made for my friends. What
about my
autobiography? Couldn't
you find the details
of my life
engaging
even for the space of a letter? When I

was a little girl, I wanted the bees
to sit on the yellow satin ribbons
combed into my blond braids,
and sometimes they did. I felt chosen
and would smile, nod my head:
the bee goddess.
But other children
ran away. "She has bees on her head!" they'd scream.
Cassandra, I was, even then.

Beauty

FOR TIM LANE

I never thought of him as beautiful,
but today he looked as tired as if he had fought a forest fire
    all night,
and he made me want to hand him a hot paper cup
of fire-fighting coffee,
though I know actually that he never drinks
that brew.
He's worried about
their car
that needs replacing,
and is exhausted as much from the stationhouse tedium
of being a house husband,
taking care of a toddler,
and the candleflame wish
that his wife, a special ed teacher, didn't always
get assigned the worst, most incendiary jobs because
of her expertise.
He wants to tend her, even light a bonfire for her,
but working part time as a janitor
while he earns
a Master's degree, being a full-time
new father, knowing they can't
afford to replace their car which is almost totally
burned out and ready for the junkyard
gives him that look.

Yet he smiles at me, listens
to my tales filled with hot air,
and lovingly receives the gift of my fiery criticism.
He knows the disappointments
of the auto assembly line, his father a frequently
laid-off mechanic who still sent him through college on a blue collar
    ticket.
How I have always admired this man,
yet never seen him as beautiful—

his red-headed Irish grin, a rainy-day grin.
His fire, more like
a steady pilot light that almost no one but
the repairman ever sees. But today
his face seemed beautiful in its everyday fatigue.
He wore a blue mechanic's shirt
with a name, not his, on the pocket,
and he paced the room when I suggested ways to change a letter
he'd written. "I can't,
I don't want to
sell myself," he says. I smile and rewrite the paragraph for him.
After all, there are fires that are invisible and useful
and more important than those big ones
    often burning out of control,
        destroying acres of forest
           and all the houses, spotted owls and deer in their
              paths.
I think I saw that pilot light
glowing out of his face today,
keeping the stove ready for a meal
or the water tank full of hot water,
or the furnace ready to remove autumn's chill.

It surprised me,
fire-observer that I am,
that I had never seen it before.

Photo by KEVA Partnership

Jan Worth

Jan Worth (b. 1949) teaches writing at the University of Michigan-Flint. She has a bachelor's degree in journalism from Kent State University, a master's degree in social work from the University of Michigan, and a master of fine arts in poetry from Warren Wilson College. Her poems, essays, short stories, and reviews have been published in many magazines and newspapers, including the *Michigan Quarterly Review, Passages North,* the *MacGuffin,* the *Detroit Free Press,* and the *Flint Journal.* In 1996, her poem *Why We Love Men Dancing* won the *MacGuffin* Magazine National Poet Hunt. She is writing a novel based on her experiences as a Peace Corps volunteer, and has spent two residencies so far at the Ragdale Foundation. Worth lives in Flint with her husband, poet Danny Rendleman.

Late Raking

FOR MY FATHER

So this is what passes for sun in late November,
silver gray and urgent. This is what we get,
all we can expect or hope for: the relief of black branches.
Finally, all the leaves are down. I rake a mangle of stick
and leaf and divots of moss. I am industrious,
that Midwest virtue. I rake to see the black dirt show,
the cleanliness of it, courting an urge toward heavy freeze,
this crunchy blackness before the snow.

One Sunday like this in the Fifties my father lost faith,
blessed the body of Christ and wanted another woman,
touched three hundred hands at the sanctuary door
and, later, at our dark table, tore apart my mother's
fried chicken and explained once again about hermaneutics
and the three important points of rhetoric. That once he wanted
out, but the heavy woodwork of God pinned him down.

Looking back at home, the spareness I've eked out
pleases me, frostbitten morning glories cut away
from squared concrete and tough pale grass.
August's lush herbs shrivel, and the cat gnaws
dried up catnip twigs. This was my childhood:
scraped yards ready for winter, tidy and desolate,
the riot of autumn hushed up fast, busheled and burned.
But the body warms to this. All these leopard-spotted
leaves, color merging into humus, the seductive smell
of hibernation or hay rides. I understand why
the cat rolls in the damp black unearthed by raking.

That year my mother often said, breathe deep!
Her love of breathing—or was it the duty of breathing—
stays with me now. The love I put in later, when
I wanted her happy. I give her pleasures she never
dreamed of. No, it is me who loves to breathe
the frigid outdoor air, gulping it.

Wolf Moon Morning

Kitchen windows today:
chiseled triptych of ebony
against blue, the trees Japanese
in their taut hysteria against
the dawn, stripped branches
stretched up like black ballerinas.

Here inside, where winter
is art, the earnest radio
orates on, repeating itself,
a seismograph without a quake.
Snow lands like gauze
on a chilblain. It's so dry
dead squirrel bones crack in the woods,
collapsing beneath their musty pelts.
In the crisp leafbeds, tulip bulbs twist
microscopically closer, in a tropism
of warmth, toward each other.

Planning for Paris, First Time

I have to start now
getting ready for Paris.

My husband will wish
he is younger there.
I'll need to be as pretty
as life permits. I think
of contacts, so, when he looks
at me across the cafe table
on various romantic rues,
my eyes will glow with
their natural intelligence.

I hope he'll be glad I'm there
when he sees the long legs
and tawny biceps of Paris,
the unlined elbows of the girls.

I hope when we stroll through the Louvre
he will love my insights, and my hair
which I'm growing for the occasion.
I want to occupy his mind, back in
our "better" hotel, like the Mona Lisa.
I want him to want my arms around him
more than Venus de Milo's.

And if we find a jazz joint with a few
expatriates or cool Pierres skulking
and smoking and talking about
Truffaut and Poe and Columbo,
I want to be at my wittiest,
bon mots twinkling out of me
like a psilocybin dream.

My husband will say, why
didn't I do this before?—
the immensity of his regrets
haunting him through
the picturesque alleys
and the Champs Elysee and
he'll want to stay forever.
Rain on Montmartre will seem sad,
and the act of breaking apart
a single crispy baguette
will be momentous.

I have to start now
getting ready for Paris.

Why We Love Men Dancing

Men dancing show their curves—
the female side that comes as welcome news.
After sensuous beaujolais and cognac-flavored
small cigars shared across the table,
after the red rug is rolled up
from the oak floor, the men soften
around the music. They let their heavy heads
loose; the muscles around the thick jugulars
visibly slacken, releasing the brain
and its tense defenses. These are not
men celebrating the kill, but those joyful
in ending the bloodbath. These men
have hips that sway into an "s,"
the "s" open both ways with equal grace,
and after the living room dance
their undulant arms are defter,
able to embrace the women,
who are right there waiting, smiling
through our own earthly motions.

Anne Ohman Youngs

Anne Ohman Youngs has three chapbooks: *Markers* (1988), *A Bracelet of Mouse Hands* (1995), and *Thirty Octaves above Middle C* (1998). Her poems appear in anthologies and numerous literary journals, such as *Cream City Review, Mid-American Review,* the *Connecticut Review,* and the *Midwest Quarterly.* One of the founders of the literary journal *Passages North,* Youngs currently serves as its poetry editor. She lives in Escanaba, Michigan, and teaches writing at Northern Michigan University in Marquette.

X and Y

When the TV coaxed me to order a Bedazzler
so I could punch fake gems
and metal dots into my clothes
and be the hit of every party,
I almost bought it—maybe because
I've read all the fairytales
and sometimes want the ease of believing
things stand for something, like that mind tattoo
biology is destiny.

I'm always waiting for some kind of
precise vision that explodes those
programmed-in connections, all that status quo.
And there's always some confusion—for instance,
I still don't understand the *x* and *y*
in an algebraic equation,
or the lily and death, such flair
holding something dark and narrow. But I know
I want to drape myself in a beaded curtain,
cut my hair to its roots

and hit the streets, quit planting
my father's idea of a garden, the one he said
needed taut strings down each row
and neat "v's" for seed he'd drop in
while pointing at the envelopes'
peas, corn, and yellow beans.
This is what it's all about, he'd say,
this is what it all means—dirt to green,
meaning, of course, *grief to money.*

And I believed him
the way I believed my mother
who praised my bowls full of shelled peas
or armsful of corn.
Angels and harps, she'd say, *angels and harps.*
Some day the Blessed Virgin will send you
4 healthy children—born to it,

the laced-in waistline, breasts mounding
above a push-up bra. First
the short red dresses and black spike heels,
then the long white dress, and the veil
I should be able to see through—Snow White,
Cinderella, The Princess and the Pea:
        purity and reward,
        self-sacrifice, reward,
        soft skin, reward.

The unknown *x* and *y*? They're waiting.
Dark configurations in an 8th-grade algebra book.
Ciphers scratched on those minutes
the teacher spent staring at the girls' breasts.
I'm still trying to figure it all out,
maybe grasp the *y*'s stem
and, like a diviner, a water-witch,
aim it at the ground to see whatever it is
my neighbor's grandchild saw yesterday

when she pulled a red snapdragon
out of my garden, put it in her mouth
and chewed. She didn't know
she was breaking the rules
about someone else's garden,
or maybe practicing for the future
when her parents tell her *No*
and she places it between her lips,
lights it, and sends it up in smoke.

How to Draw a Crow

Ahead are frozen fields and a car parked at the roadside, its trunk gaping and rust puncturing a wired door. The driver shuffles over crusty snow toward a deer hit by some earlier car or truck. He slips on steaming entrails and breaks the snow as he bends to lift and examine the hind legs.

Beside a gravel road, his three children wait for a school bus. They never play parcheesi or fold origami, and when the blowing snow speaks, they don't hear it above their voices choked with wood smoke. In the house behind them, their mother, wearing long gray socks with holes, brushes crumbs and carries chipped plates to the kitchen sink. Her mornings match her afternoons and evenings perfectly.

Bobbing his head up and down, the man follows his footsteps back to the car, removes an axe and tests its edge with his thumb. Now do you understand the crow? Can you draw it with your pencil? Fill it in with that kind of happiness?

Losing It

"The only inborn urges we have left are fear of falling and fear of loud noises."

John Watson, behavioral psychologist

I'd just like to understand anything tonight,
like why, when he knows my smells belong,
my landlord's dog wanders in to sniff my room,
and why,

when a friend tells me
he has to fight the urge
to flip his electric razor's "on" switch
and toss it in his bathwater,

I pat his shoulder and say,
Yeah . . . yeah, I know what you mean . . .
when I want to say, *Please! Don't tell me this.*
I'm as helpless as you.

A lot of what I do
occurs in direct proportion to what people
don't say to me and what I don't say to them,
and I can't depend on smell

to warn me to lower my head, growl,
and back out of a room, any more than,
after years of figuring the occasional lone goose
must be sad and lonely,

I can't be sure he isn't happy
to be away from a noisy gang
that elbows him around, like the guy who left
the card game downstairs, yelling,
Lousy cards, no more booze . . .I'm outta here!

And, if two people stand under
a neon Exit sign, does this mean the end
of the movie? That one with the couple

who try to make love
in a hammock and wind up screaming
at each other because all they do
is sag interstitially?

Or, despite passion's early promise, maybe
after a certain amount of time spent stuck
head-first in its cadmium and selenium,
we come to that place

where some inner state
we might, once, have relied on,
stiff-arms us and, at a speed
some 30 octaves above middle C, takes off.

Tribute to
Four Michigan Poets

Philip Legler (1928–1992)

Phil Legler started his journey toward Michigan when he graduated from Denison University in 1950 and then took his MFA from the State University of Iowa in 1953. From the beginning, his love of teaching and his desire to write took him through a series of prestigious teaching positions, including stints at Ohio University, Illinois Wesleyan, and Sweet Briar College. Finally, in 1968 he was hired to teach in the English department at Northern Michigan University in Marquette, where his skill and reputation made him a much sought-after professor.

From Marquette he wrote poems celebrating the Upper Peninsula landscape, and clear-voiced, evocative love poems, publishing his work in such notable publications as *Poetry,* the *Paris Review,* and *Prairie Schooner.* He was widely read throughout Michigan and his poems often found their way into *Passages North,* where he became an eloquent, haunting voice for the lost, quieter places of northern Michigan. His publishing career also included three full-length collections of poems: *A Change of View* (University of Nebraska Press, 1964), *The Intruder* (University of Georgia Press, 1972), and *North Country Images* (privately printed, 1988).

Many Michigan writers were lucky to find their way onto his Christmas card list, and every year from 1963 until 1990 Phil would faithfully write and send a Christmas greeting via his yearly postcard. Phil died in 1992 and is survived by his wife, Martha, whom he married in 1950, and three children, Amy, Barbara, and David.

How to Keep Warm

Winter is here again, deep snow
covering the grass. In the snowfield
now, once daisies even in late fall,
the wind blows me backwards, facing
the slough. Up to my crotch in snow,
I turn back, thinking of snowshoes,
how I will walk out the way a man

gives himself up to it, leaving
his tracks behind. The tracks that pad
back to camp remember. Like the night-
fire dead in the fireplace, I had not
thought of until it was gone. Over-
head a gull dips, searching for food.
How to keep warm! In town they pack

rooms, snow tunnels in the yards.
Weeks ago when the cold began, we kept
our hands inside our coat pockets,
soft as the nests squirrels build to
survive. They have stored their acorns.
The ice on the slough builds ten inches
thick and stops, blocked at the lake,
ice-caps jutting up. And so I turn,
retracing my steps as I've done all along.

Lawrence Pike (1932–1995)

Lawrence Pike was born in Detroit in 1932 and raised in Saginaw, Michigan. A graduate of the University of Michigan and Wayne State University, he wrote and taught in the Detroit area for over thirty years, most recently at Macomb County Community College, where he taught composition, poetry, and contemporary literature. His work was published in *Green River Review, 5 a.m., Passages North, University of Windsor Review*, and *River Styx* and anthologized in *Michigan Hot Apples, Passages North Anthology, Still Life with Conversation,* and *Contemporary Michigan Poetry: Poems from the Third Coast* (1988).

His books of poetry and prose were published as *Now that Good Jack Armstrong's Gone, Hideout Matinees,* and *Pierced by Sound* with the Fallen Angel Press and Ridgeway Press. *Hideout Matinees's* popularity demanded a second printing. Jack Zucker had this to say while reviewing his work for the *Birmingham Eccentric:* "Pike writes with a directness and honesty that make the reader expect a good deal of emotional mayhem. But humor is an integral component of Pike's impersonal poems, and toughness of the others. Sometimes, he rhymes and sometimes he writes free verse but anything written by Lawrence Pike sounds only like him and his city, Detroit."

He received a Creative Artist Award from the Michigan Council for the Arts and was Writer-in-Residence for the Creative-Writers-in-the-Schools program. He also enjoyed time as Poet-in-Residence at the prestigious Ragdale Foundation in Lake Forest, Illinois, where work for *Pierced by Sound* was completed. His was a life of writing and teaching. Myriad students are grateful for his time and kindness that helped their own writing blossom. He was also a tireless supporter of readings and writers in Michigan. His writing spanned four decades. It is difficult to choose a single poem to represent the rich legacy of his work. However, perhaps Thornton Wilder is correct when he states in *Our Town* that one can return on some favorite day. With that in mind, we chose the following work from *Pierced by Sound.*

From My Journal

I sat with Howard Koch, the writer. Remember
him? He wrote our best-known lines:
Here's looking at you, kid, and
Play it Sam, play our song.
Sat, I say, with Howard Koch and his wife Annie
drinking cocktails with my then-wife Janet.
Sat with this man,
his collar up (he's in his eighties)
his liquor fine, (ah, scotch with Koch)
and talked of what the agents want now
and the blacklist he was on with Annie once.
And then he asked about my work. Sweetest man!
I told him I still had hopes that . . .
But no matter. What I mean to say is
even should we forget his name
here's-looking-at-you looked at me, said Play it, Larry,
while streams babbled, while I sipped his spirits,
as I touched a woman's arm.
Certain days where do they amble?
give heart to us all.

Stephen Tudor (1933–1994)

Stephen Tudor was an editor of the Hundred Pound Press, an associate professor of English at Wayne State University, and an avid sailor. He received a National Endowment for the Arts Fellowship in 1987 for poetry and a Creative Artist Grant from the Michigan Council for the Arts.

His work was widely published in literary magazines such as the *American Poetry Review, Iowa Review, North American Review,* and *Michigan Quarterly Review* and was anthologized in *Contemporary Michigan Poetry: Poems from the Third Coast* (1988). His book *Hangdog Reef* was published in 1989 and another, *Haul-Out,* in 1996, posthumously, both by Wayne State University Press.

His interest in the Great Lakes began in 1979, when he acquired a twenty-five-foot wooden sloop, Fortsma, shortly after he and his family moved to Detroit. His backyard opened onto the Detroit River, from where he would often sail to Canada and beyond. Interviewed with Alice Fulton on the television program *Couplets* in 1990, Stephen admitted that his avocation echoed a natural resonance with poetry.

About *Haul-Out,* Robert Dana's review states: "Sailing has become for Steve the catalyst of his personal deepening as well as the subject matter and driving force of his best poems. Now, in . . . *Haul-Out* we see the poems blossom into another dimension. . . . There is now a vision of the dark end of all journeying." But perhaps Daniel Hughes characterized this symbiosis best in the following excerpt from the foreword of *Haul-Out:* "When Steve Tudor lost his life sailing on the Great Lakes in 1994, his friends and readers knew it would not be 'o.k.' and that the 'reassurances' would probably never come. But the poems he left behind . . . give us solace and a memory and remind us, in the words of Wallace Stevens, how poetry helps us to live our lives. . . ."

Because he is no longer with us, it is tempting to overemphasize the deep elegiac note in his work, but the archetype of the doomed poet-sailor is irresistible. We do not think of the drowned Hart Crane or Shelley as victims of accident but rather as fulfillers of their destinies. The sailor-poet tempts the cruel muses: he lives near the beginning of things and courts their end as well. But this elegiac impulse in Tudor is both resisted and embraced.

Steve Tudor came upon his "impossible weather," but the existence of these bracing poems makes us feel, in an ironic yet strengthening way, that he survived it.

Haul-Out

It's haul-out day, later in the season
than is good for the boat or me. I rig
a gin pole, tie halyards and stays back
and pull the mast, careful not to smash
antenna or vane coming down. Snow flurries,
glazes on puddles, this is the month of storms,
vessels iced-over at mid-lake. Sure I give
thanks for the luck I've had, for you
especially: for summer and sunlight, and
there she hangs in her slings. I raise her,
take a brush to her, cleanse her of algae and
sediments, wash away my own season's sins.

It's only my life, this banged up, obsolete
plastic heap with its faded gelcoat, frayed lines
and . . . poor me. And we'd engaged so intensely,
skin, hair, teeth, nails, the roots of the flesh,
it barely seemed I'd the strength to make it
to Bristol, and now it's come time for hanging it up,
tanks cleared, engine drained, compartments
left open to air, and then the canvas
to tent us against the impossible weather.

John Woods (1926–1995)

John Woods attended Indiana University on the GI Bill, studying physics at first, but then switching to English when, as an undergraduate, his poems were accepted for publication in the *Atlantic Monthly* and the *Kenyon Review.* He won a scholarship to the Iowa Writers Workshop in 1958–59 and then taught at Western Michigan University from 1959 until his retirement in 1992, encouraging other poets, both students and colleagues, and publishing his own skillful, lyrical, hard-edged poems in *Poetry, Paris Review, Poetry Northwest, Field, Ploughshares,* and dozens of other journals. He won both the Theodore Roethke Award and the Helen Bullis Award from *Poetry Northwest* and two Borestone Poetry Awards. His poems were collected in nine volumes, from *The Deaths at Paragon,* Indiana (Indiana University Press) in 1955 to *Black Magnolias* (University Press of Florida) in 1994. He was the first faculty member to be named Distinguished Faculty Scholar at Western Michigan, and his work was recognized by a Distinguished Michigan Artist Award and a Fellowship from the National Endowment for the Arts. Some of his most personal and most moving poems appeared in *Black Magnolias* just a year before his death. "Cleave unto Me" is from the extraordinary final section of that book.

Cleave unto Me

Cleave unto me,
body to body, mind to mind,
laugh with me at the absurdities
as our halt lives stumble.

I must feel like soil
that slips through the fingers
in the Aprils, the Mays, all the days
that made the hands tingle.

Cleave unto me,
though I burn rust on your metals.
I would be the earth that curls back
from the harrow and not lie fallow.

I want to be the bed where you put in
your roses. When I rise up lushly,
I want to be taken to your dark alcove
and burn in your vase.

Grateful acknowledgment is made for permission to reprint the following poems in this volume:

Priscilla Atkins
"The Spanish Professor"—*Cream City Review*
"The Boy Who Loved Butterflies"—*William and Mary Review*
"Gifts from Meiling"—*Nebraska Review*
"Watching for Meteors on Nestucca Bay"—*Cream City Review*

Nick Bozanic
"Conversion"—*The Long Drive Home*, Anhinga Press, 1989
"At Slea Head, County Kerry, Spring"—*This Once: Poems 1976–1996*, Anhinga Press, 1997
"The Heron"—*This Once: Poems 1976–1996*
"The Mourning Dove"—*This Once: Poems 1976–1996*

Anthony Butts
"Angels"—*Fifth Season*, New Issues Press, 1997, and *Giant Steps: The New Generation of African American Writers*, William Morrow & Co., 2000
"Yellow Archipelago"—*The Watershed Anthology*, vol. 1, no. 1, University of Wisconsin-La Crosse, and *Callaloo*
"A Poe Story"—*Fifth Season*, *Giant Steps: The New Generation of African American Writers*, *Crab Orchard Review* 2, no. 2 (under the title "Coasters"), *American Poetry: The Next Generation*, Carnegie Mellon University Press, 2000
"Detroit, City of Straits"—*Fifth Season*
"Machines"—*Giant Steps: The New Generation of African American Writers*, and *Callaloo*

Gladys Cardiff
"Beautiful Zombies"—*A Bare Unpainted Table*, New Issues Press, 1999
"Khv:na"—*A Bare Unpainted Table*
"Last Days at Petland on Aurora Avenue"—*A Bare Unpainted Table*
"Definition of Space: Giacometti, 1901–1966"—*A Bare Unpainted Table*

Michael Delp
"The River Inside"—*The Coast of Nowhere*, Wayne State University Press, 1998
"The River Everywhere"—*The Coast of Nowhere*

Stuart Dybek
"Windy City"—*Poetry International*
"Today, Tonight"—*Poetry*
"Overhead Fan"—*Poetry*
"Inspiration"—*TriQuarterly*

Nancy Eimers
"Unplugged"—*No Moon*, Purdue University Press, 1997
"Exam"—*No Moon*
"Arlington Street"—*Indiana Review* and *The New Breadloaf Anthology of Contemporary American Poetry*, New England Press, 1999

Linda Nemec Foster
"Amber Necklace from Gdansk"—*Poet Lore*
"Dancing with My Sister"—*Witness* and *Century of Voices*, Detroit Women Writers, 1999
"Our Last Day in Krakow"—*Poet Lore*

Alice Fulton
"Call The Mainland"—*Postmodern Culture*
"Failure"—*TriQuarterly*
"Close"—*Denver Quarterly* and *A Visit to the Gallery*, University of Michigan Museum of Art, 1997

Mary Jo Firth Gillett
"Word"—*Harvard Review*
"Spindrift"—*Crab Orchard Review*
"Memory"—*Sycamore Review*
"World Enough"—*Michigan Quarterly Review*
"In the Spectrum of Light"—*Passages North*

Linda Gregerson
"For the Taking"—*Atlantic Monthly* and *The Woman Who Died in Her Sleep*, Houghton Mifflin, 1996
from "The Woman Who Died in Her Sleep"—*Yale Review* and *The Woman Who Died in Her Sleep*
"Fish Dying on the Third Floor at Barneys"—*Ploughshares* and *The Woman Who Died in Her Sleep*

Robert Haight
"This River"—*Northeast*
"Fish Flies"—*Controlled Burn*
"Two Dogs with Children"—*Joyride*

Jim Harrison
from "Geo-Bestiary"—*Collected Poems*, Copper Canyon Press, 1998

Bob Hicok
"Building a Painting a Home"—*Iowa Review* and *Pushcart Prize XXIV*
"Plus Shipping"—*Shenandoah* and *Plus Shipping*, BOA Editions, 1998
"Other Lives and Dimensions and Finally a Love Poem"—*The Journal* and *Plus Shipping*
"Finally I Buy X-Ray Glasses"—*Southern Review*

Conrad Hilberry
"The Expatriates"—*Gettysburg Review* and *Player Piano*, Louisiana State University Press, 1999
"Lullaby after the Rain"—*Snowy Egret* and *Player Piano*
"Macabre"—*Gettysburg Review* and *Player Piano*
"Qui Tollis Peccata Mundi"—*Third Coast* and *Player Piano*

Patricia Hooper
"In the Backyard"—*Ploughshares* and *At the Corner of the Eye*, Michigan State University Press, 1997
"The Gardener"—*American Scholar*
"Diligence"—*At the Corner of the Eye*
"Monet's Garden"—*At the Corner of the Eye*

Jonathan Johnson
"Retirement"—*Indiana Review*
"510"—*Alaska Quarterly*

Arnold Johnston
"Spectators as We Are"—*Embers*
"Syzygy in Center Field"—*Passages North*

Laura Kasischke
"Cocktail Waitress"—*Fire and Flower*, Alice James Books, 1998
"My Heart"—*Fire and Flower*

Josie Kearns
"Quaro"—*Poetry Northwest*
"Xelah Xalong"—*Poetry Northwest*
"Hystra"—*Poetry Northwest*

David Dodd Lee
"Death on U.S. 131"—*Downsides of Fish Culture*, New Issues Press, 1997

"A Poem about Blue Gills"—*Sycamore Review* and *Downsides of Fish Culture*
"Three Stories about Owls"—*Downsides of Fish Culture*

Philip Legler
"How to Keep Warm"—*Passages North*

Thomas Lynch
"An Evening Walk to the Sea By Friesians"—*Still Life in Milford,* Norton, 1998
"Bishop's Island"—*Still Life in Milford*
"The Old Operating Theatre, London"—*Still Life in Milford*
"*Still Life in Milford*—Oil on Canvas by Lester Johnson"—*Still Life in Milford*

Naomi Long Madgett
"Packrat"—*Exits and Entrances*, Lotus Press, 1978
"On Corcovado Mountain"—*Octavia and Other Poems,* Third World Press, 1988
"Reluctant Light"—broadside by Lotus Press
"'The Sun Do Move'"—*Octavia and Other Poems*
"Renewal"—broadside by Lotus Press

Peter Markus
"Brothers"—*MacGuffin*
"Light"—*Prose Poem: An International Journal*
"Black Light"—*Prose Poem: An International Journal*
"On Becoming a Bird"—*Third Coast*

David Marlatt
"Horse Hair Mattress"—*A Hog Slaughtering Woman*, New Issues Press, 1996
"Trout"—*A Hog Slaughtering Woman*
"Spring Thaw"—*A Hog Slaughtering Woman*
"Dahlias"—*A Hog Slaughtering Woman*
"A Hog Slaughtering Woman"—*A Hog Slaughtering Woman*

Joseph Matuzak
"Rust"—Eating Fire, Ridgeway Press, 2000
"Poaching with Darby and Happy Harry"—*Eating Fire*
"Eating Fire"—*Eating Fire*
"The Size of Heaven"—*Eating Fire*
"'I with no rights in the matter'"—*Eating Fire*

Kathleen McGookey
"Honeymoon"—*Field*
"Last Night, an Owl"—*Field*

Judith Minty
"Deer at the Door"—*Controlled Burn*
"The Language of Whales"—*Poems for the Wild Earth*

Thylias Moss
"The Limitation of Beautiful Recipes"—*Last Chance for the Tarzan Holler*, Persea Books, 1998
"The Right Empowerment of Light"—*Last Chance for the Tarzan Holler*
"A Hot Time in a Small Town"—*Last Chance for the Tarzan Holler*

Julie Moulds
"Renoir's Bathers"—*The Woman with a Cubed Head*, New Issues Press, 1998
"Rapture Three"—*The Woman with a Cubed Head*

William Olsen
"Paradise, Michigan"—*Vision of a Storm Cloud*, TriQuarterly Books: Northwestern University
     Press, 1996
"In the Time of Blithe Astonishments"—*Vision of a Storm Cloud*
"The Fold-Out Atlas of the Human Body"—*Hayden's Ferry Review*

Anne-Marie Oomen
"What I Learned at 'Down the Road' Café"—*The Lucid Stone*
"Because This Did Not Happen to Me"—*Prairie Hearts: Women View the Midwest*, Outrider
  Press, 1996
"Awakening"—*Borderlands: Texas Poetry Review*

John Palen
"When You Finish Your First Real Poem"—*Birmingham Poetry Review*, Mayapple Press, 1997
"Sirens"—Mayapple Press
"Slice of Life"—Mayapple Press

Rosalie Sanara Petrouske
"Moon through an Amber Glass"—*Southern Poetry Review*
"A Postcard from My Mother"—*Dancing Shadow Review* and *1994 Grolier Poetry Prize
  Anthology*, Grolier Poetry Bookstore, 1994
"Angels"—in "A Poem in a Pamphlet Series," Andrew Mountain Press, 1997

Lawrence Pike
"From My Journal"—*Pierced by Sound,* Ridgeway Press, 1991

Susan Blackwell Ramsey
"Aftereffects of Bell's Palsy"—*Primavera*
"Metonomy"—*Studio Potter*

Greg Rappleye
"Charon in August"—*Sycamore Review*
"Terrible"—*Southern Review*

Danny Rendleman
"Cheese Lines, Flint, Michigan"—*Passages North* and *The Middle West*, Ridgeway Press, 1995

Jack Ridl
"First Cut"—*Poetry East* and *Full Court*, Breakaway Books, 1996
"Against Elegies"—*Poetry*

John Rybicki
"Becoming"—*The Quarterly* and *Traveling at High Speeds*, New Issues Press, 1996
"Begin"—*Field*
"King"—*Northwest Review*
"Interlochen Center for the Arts"—*Quarterly West*

Herbert Scott
"The Blue Turtle"—*Poetry East*
"Bees"—*Michigan Quarterly Review*
"Mime"—*Michigan Quarterly Review*
"The Most Terrible and Beautiful Thing"—*Poetry Northwest*

Heather Sellers
"Widow's Peak"—*Hawaii Review*
"Polar"—*Field*
"Girlfriend"—*The Women's Review of Books*

Diane Seuss
"Kansas"—*It Blows You Hollow*, New Issues Press, 1998
"Houseboy"—*Poetry Northwest*
"Rising"—*It Blows You Hollow*

Faith Shearin
"Entropy"—*Alaska Quarterly Review*
"Desire"—*Shankpainter*
"Luck"—*Chicago Review*
"Ruins"—*Ploughshares*

"Matrimony"—*New York Quarterly*

Marc J. Sheehan
"Thanksgiving"—*MacGuffin*
"The Off Season"—*Sky*
"Second Marriage"—*Sky*

Joseph Sheltraw
"The White Kid"—*Aethlon: The Journal of Sport Literature*
"Carnival Worker"—*The Driftwood Review*
"Boys in Boxing Poses"—*Gulf Stream Magazine*
"Epilogues from Seven Unsuccessful Stories about My Father"—*Sou'wester*

F. Richard Thomas
"The Last Cherry Bomb"—*Driftwood Review*
"Death at Camp Pahoka"—*Miracles,* Canoe Press, 1996

Richard Tillinghast
"Father in October"—*New Republic*
"His Days"—*New Yorker*
"A Morning"—*Gettysburg Review*
"Tea"—*Kenyon Review*

Rodney Torreson
"When the Babe Stormed New York"—*Giants Play Well in the Drizzle*
"Wooden Ducks"—*Northeast*
"Ties"—*Northeast*
"Maris and Dylan Came Scowling Out of Hibbing, Minnesota"—*Elysian Field*

Stephen Tudor
"Haul-Out"—*Haul-Out: New and Selected Poems,* Wayne State University Press, 1996

Robert VanderMolen
"In February"—*Jejune*
"Outside of Town"—*Artful Dodge*
"Painting Shutters"—*Grand Street*
"Bodies"—*Grand Street*
"Miles Davis"—*Jejune*
"Making a Fire"—*Artful Dodge* and *Peaches,* Sky Press, 1998

Diane Wakoski
"Blue Nails"—*Argonaut Rose,* Black Sparrow Press, 1998
"Costa Rican Coffee"—*Argonaut Rose*
"Wanting Bees"—*Argonaut Rose*
"Beauty"—*Argonaut Rose*

John Woods
"Cleave unto Me"—*Black Marigolds,* University Press of Florida, 1994

Jan Worth
"Wolf Moon Morning"—*MacGuffin*
"Planning for Paris, First Time"—*Swinging Girl,* Carol Love Press, 1996
"Why We Love Men Dancing"—*Swinging Girl*

Anne Ohman Youngs
"X and Y"—*Connecticut Review*
"Losing It"—*Eleventh Muse*

Titles in the Great Lakes Books Series

Life after the Line, by Josie Kearns, 1990

Michigan Lumbertowns: Lumbermen and Laborers in Saginaw, Bay City, and Muskegon, 1870–1905, by Jeremy W. Kilar, 1990

Detroit Kids Catalog: The Hometown Tourist, by Ellyce Field, 1990

Waiting for the News, by Leo Litwak, 1990 (reprint)

Detroit Perspectives, edited by Wilma Wood Henrickson, 1991

Life on the Great Lakes: A Wheelsman's Story, by Fred W. Dutton, edited by William Donohue Ellis, 1991

Copper Country Journal: The Diary of Schoolmaster Henry Hobart, 1863–1864, by Henry Hobart, edited by Philip P. Mason, 1991

John Jacob Astor: Business and Finance in the Early Republic, by John Denis Haeger, 1991

Survival and Regeneration: Detroit's American Indian Community, by Edmund J. Danziger, Jr., 1991

Steamboats and Sailors of the Great Lakes, by Mark L. Thompson, 1991

Cobb Would Have Caught It: The Golden Age of Baseball in Detroit, by Richard Bak, 1991

Michigan in Literature, by Clarence Andrews, 1992

Under the Influence of Water: Poems, Essays, and Stories, by Michael Delp, 1992

The Country Kitchen, by Della T. Lutes, 1992 (reprint)

The Making of a Mining District: Keweenaw Native Copper 1500–1870, by David J. Krause, 1992

Kids Catalog of Michigan Adventures, by Ellyce Field, 1993

Henry's Lieutenants, by Ford R. Bryan, 1993

Historic Highway Bridges of Michigan, by Charles K. Hyde, 1993

Lake Erie and Lake St. Clair Handbook, by Stanley J. Bolsenga and Charles E. Herndendorf, 1993

Queen of the Lakes, by Mark Thompson, 1994

Iron Fleet: The Great Lakes in World War II, by George J. Joachim, 1994

Turkey Stearnes and the Detroit Stars: The Negro Leagues in Detroit, 1919–1933, by Richard Bak, 1994

Pontiac and the Indian Uprising, by Howard H. Peckham, 1994 (reprint)

Charting the Inland Seas: A History of the U.S. Lake Survey, by Arthur M. Woodford, 1994 (reprint)

Ojibwa Narratives of Charles and Charlotte Kawbawgam and Jacques LePique, 1893–1895. Recorded with Notes by Homer H. Kidder, edited by Arthur P. Bourgeois, 1994, co-published with the Marquette County Historical Society

Strangers and Sojourners: A History of Michigan's Keweenaw Peninsula, by Arthur W. Thurner, 1994

Win Some, Lose Some: G. Mennen Williams and the New Democrats, by Helen Washburn Berthelot, 1995

Sarkis, by Gordon and Elizabeth Orear, 1995

The Northern Lights: Lighthouses of the Upper Great Lakes, by Charles K. Hyde, 1995 (reprint)

Kids Catalog of Michigan Adventures, second edition, by Ellyce Field, 1995

Rumrunning and the Roaring Twenties: Prohibition on the Michigan-Ontario Waterway, by Philip P. Mason, 1995

In the Wilderness with the Red Indians, by E. R. Baierlein, translated by Anita Z. Boldt, edited by Harold W. Moll, 1996

Elmwood Endures: History of a Detroit Cemetery, by Michael Franck, 1996

Master of Precision: Henry M. Leland, by Mrs. Wilfred C. Leland with Minnie Dubbs Millbrook, 1996 (reprint)

Haul-Out: New and Selected Poems, by Stephen Tudor, 1996

Kids Catalog of Michigan Adventures, third edition, by Ellyce Field, 1997

Beyond the Model T: The Other Ventures of Henry Ford, revised edition, by Ford R. Bryan, 1997

Young Henry Ford: A Picture History of the First Forty Years, by Sidney Olson, 1997 (reprint)

The Coast of Nowhere: Meditations on Rivers, Lakes and Streams, by Michael Delp, 1997

From Saginaw Valley to Tin Pan Alley: Saginaw's Contribution to American Popular Music, 1890–1955, by R. Grant Smith, 1998

The Long Winter Ends, by Newton G. Thomas, 1998 (reprint)

Bridging the River of Hatred: The Pioneering Efforts of Detroit Police Commissioner George Edwards, 1962–1963, by Mary M. Stolberg, 1998

Toast of the Town: The Life and Times of Sunnie Wilson, by Sunnie Wilson with John Cohassey, 1998

These Men Have Seen Hard Service: The First Michigan Sharpshooters in the Civil War, by Raymond J. Herek, 1998

A Place for Summer: One Hundred Years at Michigan and Trumbull, by Richard Bak, 1998

Early Midwestern Travel Narratives: An Annotated Bibliography, 1634–1850, by Robert R. Hubach, 1998 (reprint)

All-American Anarchist: Joseph A. Labadie and the Labor Movement, by Carlotta R. Anderson, 1998

Michigan in the Novel, 1816–1996: An Annotated Bibliography, by Robert Beasecker, 1998

"Time by Moments Steals Away": The 1848 Journal of Ruth Douglass, by Robert L. Root, Jr., 1998

The Detroit Tigers: A Pictorial Celebration of the Greatest Players and Moments in Tigers' History, updated edition, by William M. Anderson, 1999

Father Abraham's Children: Michigan Episodes in the Civil War, by Frank B. Woodford, 1999 (reprint)

Letter from Washington, 1863–1865, by Lois Bryan Adams, edited and with an introduction by Evelyn Leasher, 1999

Wonderful Power: The Story of Ancient Copper Working in the Lake Superior Basin, by Susan R. Martin, 1999

A Sailor's Logbook: A Season aboard Great Lakes Freighters, by Mark L. Thompson, 1999

Huron: The Seasons of a Great Lake, by Napier Shelton, 1999

Tin Stackers: The History of the Pittsburgh Steamship Company, by Al Miller, 1999

Art in Detroit Public Places, revised edition, text by Dennis Nawrocki, photographs by David Clements, 1999

Brewed in Detroit: Bernhard Stroh and the Other Detroit Brewers, by Peter H. Blum, 1999

Enterprising Images: The Goodridge Brothers, African American Photographers, 1847–1922, by John Vincent Jezierski, 2000

Detroit Kids Catalog II: The Hometown Tourist, by Ellyce Field, 2000

The Sandstone Architecture of the Lake Superior Region, by Kathryn Bishop Eckert, 2000

Expanding the Frontiers of Civil Rights: Michigan, 1948–1968, by Sidney Fine, 2000

Graveyard of the Lakes, by Mark L. Thompson, 2000

Arab Detroit: From Margin to Mainstream, edited by Nabeel Abraham and Andrew Shryock, 2000

New Poems from the Third Coast: Contemporary Michigan Poetry, edited by Michael Delp, Conrad Hilberry, and Josie Kearns, 2000